MACHINE-KNITTED FABRICS:
FELTING TECHNIQUES

MACHINE-KNITTED FABRICS:

FELTING TECHNIQUES

Janet Nabney

B.T. Batsford Ltd, London

FOR JOHN . . . . . AGAIN?!

First published 1992

© Janet Nabney 1992

Typeset by Servis Filmsetting Ltd, Manchester
and printed in Great Britain by
BPCC Hazells Ltd, Member of BPCC Ltd

Published by
B.T. Batsford Ltd
4 Fitzhardinge Street
London W1H 0AH

A catalogue record for this book is available from
the British Library

ISBN 0 7134 6505 0

Contents

Percussion Textiles

Felting is an exciting process but many people find the task daunting. I think this may be because they think of felted fabric as simply boiled wool. This is a misconception. Yarn is affected by the temperature of water, but if felt were only created by boiling wool then primitive tribesmen would never have been able to make houses of it.

Moisture *and* friction are the two most important factors in creating felt. As I discuss later in more depth (see page 15), the basic cause of felting is the frictional difference that is responsible for rootward migration of the keratin fibres under *repeated compression*. If you understand this basic process then felting in a domestic washing machine – that is, the repeated percussion of the fabrics against each other due to the rotating action of the machine – is both practical and simple.

Percussive techniques in action – double-bed fabric before and after felting

Introduction

The discovery of felt is attributed to the Asiatic nomads. There are also various references to the discovery of felt in literature, legends and myths.

It is said that Noah laid down fleece to make a soft resting place for the animals in the ark. Warmth, trampling and urine would have done the trick, and when the journey was over the floor covering had become the world's first felt rug.

Another myth from the Old Testament is concerned with one of Solomon's sons. He was a shepherd who thought that the coat of the sheep, the fleece, could provide a warm and comfortable covering if only he could discover a way of sticking the fibres together. He tried all sorts of things and in the end he jumped up and down on the fleece in a fit of despair. His tears combined with the friction did the rest, and felt was produced.

It is said that Joseph's coat of many colours might very possibly have been a felted cape.

There is also a story of the French monk, St Clement, from the eleventh century. He was attributed with the re-discovery of felt. It seems he was intending to make a long and arduous journey, so in order to make himself as comfortable as possible on the way, he stuffed wool into his sandals to prevent himself from becoming too footsore and weary. After the pilgrimage, he found two matted pads inside his sandals instead of the wool.

Earliest prehistoric findings date from the Neolithic period (6500–6300 BC) from Catal Huyuk in Turkey. Other important excavations are from the Bronze and Iron Ages, i.e. the high burial mounds in Pazyryk in the mountains of Siberia, excavated by Rudenko in 1970. The presence of frost and ice preserved these wonderful examples of felt rugs, wall carpets, covers for the body, socks, cushions, felt-covered metal rings which served as a stand for round-bottomed vessels, women's hair accessories, and other artifacts, which can now be seen in the Hermitage Museum in St. Petersburg. Most of these remains from 700–200 BC are heavily patterned. Some of the methods the felt-makers used to embellish their felt included appliqué, mosaic, inlay and embroidery.

In China c. 230 BC, warriors used felt for shields and hats, and in Tibet felt was used for plates. It must have been vital to everyday life in Central Asia, where felt houses on wheels were found.

Yurts were the name of the sites on which the nomadic tents were erected. They were made of felt stretched on a criss-crossed lattice with a diameter of 6–10 metres (20–33 ft). Wooden trunks were covered with felt, as were the floors of the tents. Felt was also used for babies' cradles.

The nomads of Central Asia today still make felt by traditional methods but techniques have been refined and perfected over the years.

Felt coats in Iran and Afghanistan are considered status symbols. They are not made from pieces of felt sewn together but are made in one piece as if a mould was used. The principles of construction can be compared to and interpreted through garments made of skin and woven cloth (Figs. 1–2). In some cases the sleeves are too stiff to be practical, so the ends are closed. Similar garments in Siberia are made from animal

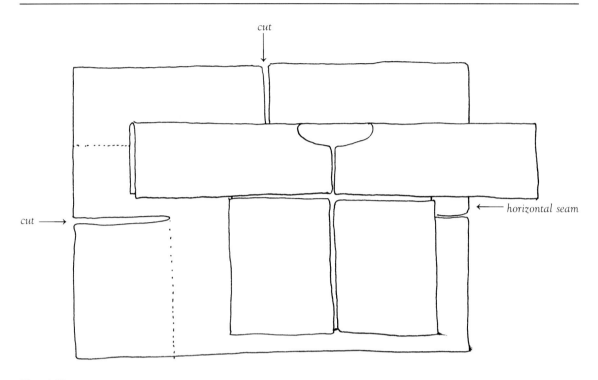

cut

horizontal seam

cut

Fig. 1 Shirt construction

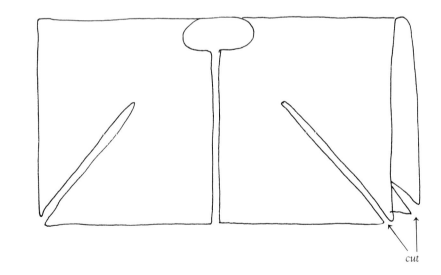

cut

Fig. 2 Coat construction

skins (deer). The size and position of horizontal slits correspond to the size and shape of a deer skin. In central Asia (Turkmen and Uzbek tribes), vestigial sleeves were tied at the back. Capes were worn over the shoulders and had slits for the arms to emerge.

In Turkey the *kepanek* is a cloak and a portable tent all rolled into one (Fig. 3). The maker marks the weight of the garment and

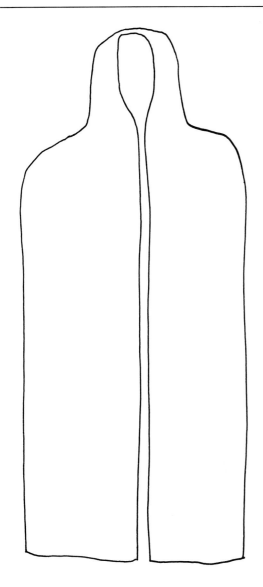

Fig. 3 One-piece coat

day. One man prepares the wool. The second man presses it into the mould. The third man puts the prepared felt form onto a wooden mould, smoothing it with a polished stone. The fourth man cuts and finishes the hat and it is then left to dry in the sun. In Turkey only Dervishes are allowed to wear felt hats!

In Ancient Greece, *pilos* meant felt. There are descriptions in the *Iliad* of felt hats. Odysseus wore a felt-lined helmet. Hesiod mentions felt in his histories, and Plato refers to felt shoes and caps. In Roman times, though, felt had fallen into disrepute and only the poorest people wore felt. Slaves, when given their freedom, were allowed to shave their heads and wear felt caps, and felt became synonymous with freedom and 'the common man'. There is evidence derived from excavations at Pompeii, that the Romans milled woollen cloths by placing them in a bowl and stamping on them with their feet to give alternate compression and relaxation. The addition of wood ash was also used to facilitate the felting process.

In his book *The Crowthers of Bankdam*, Thomas Armstrong describes a part of a cottager's cloth production:

'After the yarn were woven in the hand-loom the greasy piece, a bit at a time, were stretched out on the floor and wetted wi' piss and dung, while all the family trampled on the folds o' the cloth. The house used to stink worse than a cesspit, an' we never got rid of the smell from one week to another.'

The beret originated with the shepherds of the hills of south-west France and northern Spain (the Basque country). They knitted these caps very loosely and then these were thoroughly wetted and stretched over stones and pummelled to encourage them into the familiar beret shape. A similar

his traditional mark by inlaying coloured felt pieces into the groundwork.

Hats are made by pressing fleece into a metal dish using the hands and the feet. In Shiraz, four men can make ten hats in one

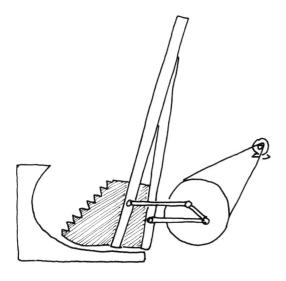

Fig. 4 Waulking mill

practice was followed in Scotland. Coarse fleeces which were unsuitable for weaving were spun and knitted on coarse needles. The completed garments or caps were then pounded in water to shrink and thicken the fabric. This process was known as *waulking* and could be done in a water-powered **waulking mill** (Fig. 4). Then they were dried to shape, teazled to raise the nap, and trimmed with shears. In the seventeenth century a large bonnet could weigh as much as 18 oz, knitted in one piece and heavily waulked. The bonnet was a solid and durable headcovering. It went out of style in Europe in the 1600s but remained popular in Scotland although it was worn primarily by the poorer folk.

The Pacific Islanders did not use sheep fleece but contrived to make a similar type of fabric called *tapa* with the inside of the bark of the paper mulberry tree, the breadfruit tree and some types of fig tree. There is evidence to suggest that flax soaked in vinegar and salt can be pressed into 'felt' and in this form it was made into 'useful armour'.

The process of felting is called 'fulling' in America and 'milling' in Britain. The felting property of wool is due to its surface scale structure, ease of deformation and ability to recover from this deformation. The result of fulling is a dense, durable three-dimensional fabric. It is only recently that the ancient method of pounding the fibre by hand has been re-discovered as an essential element in the primitive process of feltmaking.

Basically the manufacture of felt consists of three main steps:

1 *Making the batt* This entails accumulating webs of fibre into a layer in which the fibres are not oriented in the same direction (i.e. the roots are not all facing in the same direction). The scale edges on the fibres point towards the tip and the frictional coefficient is greater when they are rubbed in the tip to root direction.

2 *Hardening* This is an intermediate step where the loose fibres are all amalgamated to produce a pad. This is done by subjecting the batt to moisture, pressure and heat.

3 *Fulling* This is the final step when the loose pad is hardened, thickened, shrunk and made firmer by rubbing and beating until the desired strength of the felted fabric is obtained.

The Processes
of Felting

The Industrial Processes of Felting

Pressed felt is one of the oldest forms of non-woven fabric. In felt the fibre is intermeshed by a combination of *mechanical work, chemical action, moisture* and *heat*. The fabric shrinks and becomes thick. The fibres matt into closely-packed masses. The outline and character of the yarn pattern in the fibre becomes indistinct and the fabric loses much of its elasticity. The surface and appearance is much altered.

The exact cause of felting is not fully understood, but it may be the result of the tension in the wool, the peculiar serrated shape of the outer layers of the fibre made by the pointed tips of the overlapping scales, and the chemical characteristics of the cystine linkages. Felting appears to take place most readily in a wool fabric when it is subjected to any treatment which causes the fabric to be repeatedly compressed and then allowed to relax when it is wet. This treatment tends to bend the fibres into loops inside the constructions and it has been suggested that felting occurs when 'travelling fibres' penetrate these loops to form knots and entanglements. Wool fibres felt more readily if the tips of the fibres are softened or the roots are hardened. Felting shrinkage is unique to wool and other animal fibres.

One definition of felt is that it is a non-woven material created by the compression of wool with the help of moist heat and rubbing but without the use of a binding compound. Wool is the only fibre with properties which enable it to be felted. However, plant, artificial, and animal fibres can be made into felt if they are mixed with wool. Felt is unspun wool (topps) that has been matted by this process. Fulling is woven or knitted fabric that is matted. The definition of fulling is to cleanse or thicken cloth. Fullers do this with 'fullers earth' (hydrous silicate of alumina), which is an absorbent type of clay used to loosen grease from fibres.

It is only recently that the ancient method of pounding the fibre has been replaced by the use of full-width roller machines which were previously used for hat bodies. These have wide vibration rollers which shrink the batting faster and more evenly. For centuries soap was used as an accelerating agent. Today acid is employed almost universally.

Fulling is carried out commercially on several different types of machine in the presence of a fairly strong *soap solution*. Sometimes the technique of *acid fulling* is used. Dilute acid replaces the soap solution. In either case mechanical action is required so the wool is subjected to the *pounding* or *fulling* action. Where soap solution (*not* caustic or sodium carbonate) is used, it is general practice to saturate the items first in a soaping machine. Often penetrating agents are added to the soap solution.

In acid fulling, synthetic detergents and penetrating agents which are stable in the presence of acid are used. This is the most rapid method and produces the lightest,

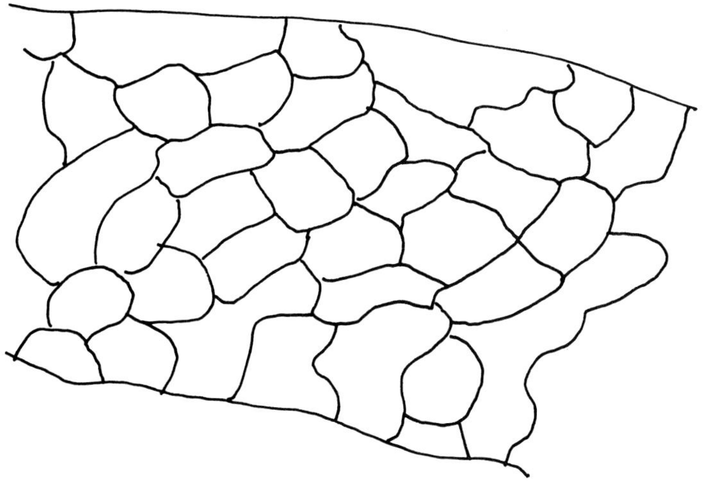

Fig. 5 Coarse scales

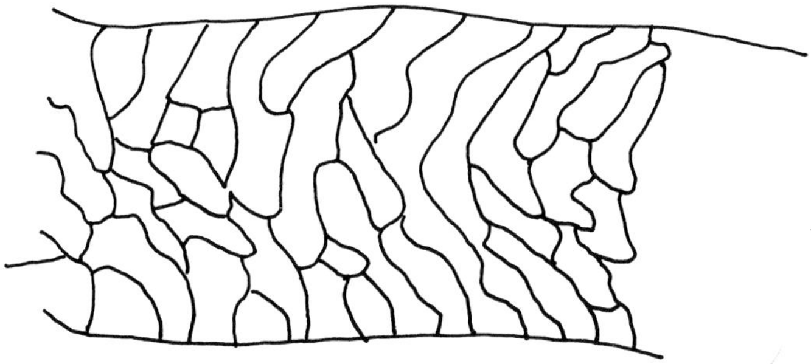

Fig. 6 Finer scales

strongest and more elastic fabrics, though the colour and 'handle' are poorer than those obtained with soap fulling. Wool is susceptible to alkali damage, but more resistant to acid than cotton or vegetable fibres.

In knitted fabrics it is generally recognized that loosely knitted constructions will be more subject to shrinkage than tight-knit constructions. The more twist there is in the yarn, the greater the relaxation in shrinkage.

Three main factors contribute to the feltability of wool, although strong boiling, dyeing or other pre-treatments can diminish this feltability.

1 *The scale-like outer structure* Friction and moisture cause the fibre to 'creep' or move backwards in a tip-to-root direction (opposite the direction in which the scales are pointing). When the fibres are massed together they curl and tangle. Heat and alkalinity (e.g. soap) increase the elasticity of the fibre so that with the added friction, pressure and moisture, the movement, shrinkage and tangling increase until the fibres mat together (Figs. 5–6). The finer fibres in a wool mix tend to intermingle more thoroughly and form an inner core. Finer and shorter fibres produce a stronger and tighter felt than coarser fibres.

2 *The crimp (or curl)* This makes the fibres more elastic. Pre-shrunk, damaged fibres will not felt. This crimp is in turn dictated by the breed, the age and the nutritional state of the sheep (and its environment), and the source of the fleece (the position on the

13

animal). The best wool comes from the rear underside of the animal. Some wools felt more readily than others, and even fibres of one type may felt to a different degree depending on their treatment. Highly crimped fibres arranged in different directions offer the best chance for felt formation.

Fig. 7 Serrated edge on scale

3 *The spiral molecular structure* Wool fibres are constructed of a series of overlapping scales that have a serrated edge (Fig. 7). A protein is present called *keratin*. This keratin has a molecular structure which give wool its elasticity or creep.

Yarns spun with a very tight twist are not very suitable for felting. A softer yarn is easier to felt. In general, fine wools produce fine, even felt and are easier to shape in three-dimensional work. Coarse wools give a firmer, harder mat and do not distort so easily. Greasy wool is difficult to felt as grease retards the felting process.

The special features that influence the felting properties of wool are the scaliness, the fibre fineness, crimp and elastic properties. Fineness and scaliness are often interrelated as the number of fibres in a given area of fabric are inversely proportional to the thickness of the fibre. The effect of crimp on felting is also important. Wools of low crimp felt more and wools of unusually high crimp felt less. Wools that have been exposed to the elements during growth felt more readily than less exposed wools but once the fibre has been made into cloth the opposite effect is noticed. That is, fabric that has been exposed to daylight for several

weeks felts much less easily than unexposed fabric. Another factor that is important in felting is plasticity. The length of the fibres is not as important. So, for example, short Merino wools mill more in woven cloths than equally fine long wools cut into similar lengths.

Felting with blends of wool and other fibres is affected by the percentage of the other fibre. The less wool there is, the less the fabric will felt. The composition or make-up of the synthetic fibre matters less than the proportion.

Types of wool that are conducive to good felting are as follows:

- *Sheep's wool*: Jacobs, Gotland, Pellssheep, Icelandic, Masham, Suffolk Cross, Shetland, Merino, Polworth, Corriedale and Corriedale/Merino. Merino wool can sometimes be difficult to felt if there is a great deal of grease present, but sprinkling it with fullers earth to remove the grease makes felting easier. These wools give a fine, even felt. Romney, Romney/Border and Leicester Cross wools also make good felt. Some more hairy yarns make a harder felt which can be useful for floor coverings.
- *Camel hair* blended with wool in the proportion 1:2 makes a good felt.
- *Cashmere* is very soft and must be blended with wool for strength.
- *Mohair* blends well with wool to make felt.
- *Alpaca* makes a very hard felt and shrinks a great deal.
- Other hairs can be blended with wool, for example *goat* and *yak*.
- *Silk* and wool blends felt well, and the silk gives the felt a sheen.
- Some natural fibres such as *flax*, *hemp*, *ramie* (Chinese linen) and *cotton* 'attach' to wool while felted but do not shrink.

The Process of Felting

The basic cause of felting is the frictional difference that is responsible for rootward migration of the keratin fibres under repeated compression. The unique property of wool is that it has the ability to migrate under mechanical action in moist conditions to form dense entanglements or felts. Wool fibres have a property known as the *directional frictional effect* (DFE). This means that there is a greater degree of friction present when the tips of the fibres are pointing in opposite directions than when they are lined up all facing the same way. It is generally believed that this is caused by the projecting tips of the scales that cover the outer sheaths of the fibres. Therefore felting is caused by a degree of irreversibility of movement of fibres in relation to each other brought about by the DFE. However, elasticity of the fibres is also important. Shrinkage is caused by the combined effects of DFE and fibre movement promoted by the elasticity of the wool. When alternately compression and relaxation are applied, the compressive force packs the fibres more tightly together and, on relaxation, the DFE prevents many of them from reverting back to their original positions. If the elasticity of the wool is reduced or removed by chemical means the fibres lose their tendency to close up. Some forms of chemical action do have a positive effect on the felting process. If the roots of the fibres are hardened or the tips softened, this will promote felting. A common practice of *carroting* was used for making hats from rabbit hairs. This involved immersing just the tips of the fibres in a solution of mercuric nitrate and nitric acid to soften them and thus promote felting.

It has also been found that the pH factor is very important in encouraging the felting process. pH is the term used to convey the measure of acidity or alkalinity of a solution. For example, vinegar (acetic acid) can be added to water to make a weak acid solutions, and washing soda can be added to make a weak alkaline solution. A solution with pH7 is considered neutral. Between pH4 and pH8 the shrinkage is lowest when the fabric is subjected to a given amount of alternating compression and relaxation (Fig. 8). (It is believed that the adjacent polypeptide chains are probably bound together by salt linkages which make the fabric more rigid, and so expansion and contraction is more difficult. This means that it is more

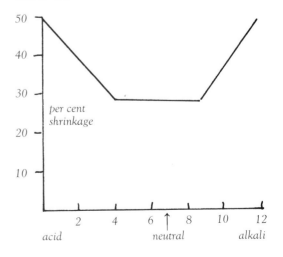

Fig. 8 The effect of pH value on felting

difficult for the fibres to form the necessary cross-links that will help them to bind together to form the mat or felt.)

The fabric must be wet in order to carry out felting because moisture interposes a dielectric film between the positive and negative charges in the salt linkages and therefore reduces the work needed for the process to occur. Soap is a good promoter of felting, not only because it is slightly alkaline but also because it seems to ease the movement of the fibres in relation to each other.

Fine wools generally felt more readily than coarser ones and there are also differences within the grades which would otherwise appear the same to the layman. The trained buyer or woolman can recognize a suitable wool by its 'feel'. If the material is held firmly in the hand and squeezed, impressions are gained of its resistance to compression and of its resilience to or recovery from compression. If the material is stroked gently one can get an impression of its smoothness or roughness, which is not to be confused with 'softness'. Both stroking and holding give impressions of warmth. There is no substitute for this acquired skill in judging fleeces for their felting suitability.

Heating wool up to 100°C (212°F) reduces its capacity to absorb moisture. At higher temperatures ammonia and hydrogen sulphide are given off. Heating, especially in the presence of moisture, reduces the breaking strength of the fibres and increases the solubility in water and mild alkali. At 150°C (302°F) woollen fibres contract in the presence of moisture.

Felting in a Domestic Washing Machine

Well now, down to the nitty-gritty. There are many misconceptions about the process of felting knitted fabric in a domestic situation. One is that you have to boil your fabric in order to achieve a felted effect. As we have seen from the previous section, the temperature of the water in the felting process is really not as important as other factors. We often obtain our yarn already spun on cones with no documentation as to its origins or the previous treatments it has been subjected to. If it is machine washable, it will not felt. So we are left with a perhaps anonymous cone of wool, and the only way to find out what sort of felted fibre it will produce and how it will react to treatment is to do samples. This may require some time and effort, but the result is worth the cost in time and money.

For those machine knitters who in the past have only knitted a garment from a reliable pattern in a branded yarn, the following procedure may seem complicated, but it is quite easy and really a great deal of fun. You do have to be fairly methodical and rather patient. But you could come up with all sorts of interesting surprises that no-one else has yet discovered.

The basic process is to knit a swatch in your chosen yarn and stitch construction, at least 100 stitches by 100 rows. Then put it into a washing machine on a normal cycle at approximately 30°C (86°F). I usually put my swatches in with any other wash I happen to be doing. Then, when you get the swatch out of the machine, you can put it into the tumble-dryer briefly (about 10 minutes will do).

Blot each swatch, lay it flat and allow it to dry. You can also 'smooth' your swatch once it is dry with a wool-hot steam iron. This serves the purpose of smoothing and 'burnishing' the surface of the felt. If you are curious about how much this particular yarn or stitch construction has been affected by the process, measure the swatch *before* you subject it to the felting procedure. However, the most important thing is to measure your swatch very carefully *after* you have washed and dried your piece of knitting.

Below are some guidelines to consider when you are designing garments which will be made up in machine-knitted, machine-felted fabric.

1 Omit seams where possible to avoid extra bulk and to ensure maximum weather-proofing.

2 Test for colour fastness as well as shrinkage.

3 Remember that large areas of colour are more effective than small intricate patterns which may get lost and amalgamate in the felting and shrinking process.

4 Try to use non-rolling (double-bed) fabric. If you are trying to felt single-bed or a rolling type of fabric this will have to be dealt with in specific ways.

5 You can sew your fabric length (not necessarily the swatch) into a tube loosely with a thin sewing cotton. The fabric will not felt to itself and can be cut apart easily when the felting is finished. This will also inhibit the natural tendency of the felt to shrink more in the centre than at the edges, which results in 'ruffling'.

6 When knitting your sample swatches it is best to use a large stitch size to allow the fabric room for friction to affect the felting process. The looser the tension, the thicker the fabric becomes.

You can give your knitted fabric a pre-treatment if you like. Excessive grease can inhibit the felting process, but on the other hand the ammonia that is present in the sweat and urine which can be found in an unwashed fleece can also make the felting process easier. To de-grease the fabric, immerse it in a warm solution of water, soap powder or detergent. Eucalyptus oil and methylated spirits are both effective in solubilizing, removing excess grease and opening the scales of the fibres. Ammonium hydroxide (household ammonia) or washing soda, soap or most detergents provide a mild alkaline solution necessary for felting to take place.

If you have a top-loading washing machine that does not 'gum-up' when pure soap is used, the recipe for felting is to fill it to a low-level setting with hand-hot (40–45°C/100–110°F) water, $\frac{1}{8}$ cup washing soda and $\frac{1}{8}$–$\frac{1}{2}$ cup of pure soap flakes. You should also add a small towel, a tennis ball, plimsoll or 'flip-flop' to provide additional abrasion. Wash the swatch for 12–15 minutes. The longer you agitate the fabric, the harder, thicker and less pliable the result will be. If you use more water you will have to increase the amount of soda and soap to $\frac{1}{4}$ cup soda and 1 cup of soap.

The general procedure for an ordinary domestic front-loading washing machine is very similar. However, it is unwise to use pure soap in these machines as it may cause some damage. You may use Sansolaine, a low-sudsing compound which has been especially designed to provide a washing solution with a pH factor suitable for producing felt in the domestic washing machine. However, you must remember to clean out the filter very carefully and frequently because you will be generating a lot of 'fluff'. It is advisable to test each swatch on various temperatures starting at 30°C (86°F). The larger the stitch size of your sample swatch, the longer the washing required and the thicker the felt will become. The cycle (or agitation) should be normal. Again, you can add a towel, a rubber plimsoll, a tennis ball or a 'flip-flop' to provide the necessary friction. A low water level also increases the agitation, as the fabric tends to float if the water level is too high.

It is unwise to try to felt a piece of knitting which is more than 12 m long.

If you need to make a felted fabric for your garment design which will finish up wider than the sample you can produce using all the needles on your machine, you will have to join together two pieces of knitting before you put them into the washing machine.

You can do this in several ways. For example:

1 Sew the two pieces together carefully by hand using a mattress stitch. Sew up with the same yarn that was used to knit the swatch.

2 Sew the two pieces together with a Hague Linker, or cast off the two pieces together on the knitting machine. Use the same yarn for the seam as was used to knit the fabric.

3 While knitting the second piece, pick up the edge of the first piece and knit it in. To do this you must pick up the 'knots' at the selvage edge of your first piece of knitting and place them onto the edge needle of the piece you are currently knitting on every alternate row.

These three methods will produce a fabric which is wider than the original piece but the seam is invisible on the right side. However, only the third method can be totally reversible. In methods 1 and 2, the seam will show up on the wrong side of your felted piece.

The Technical
Considerations of Felting
Machine-knitted Fabric

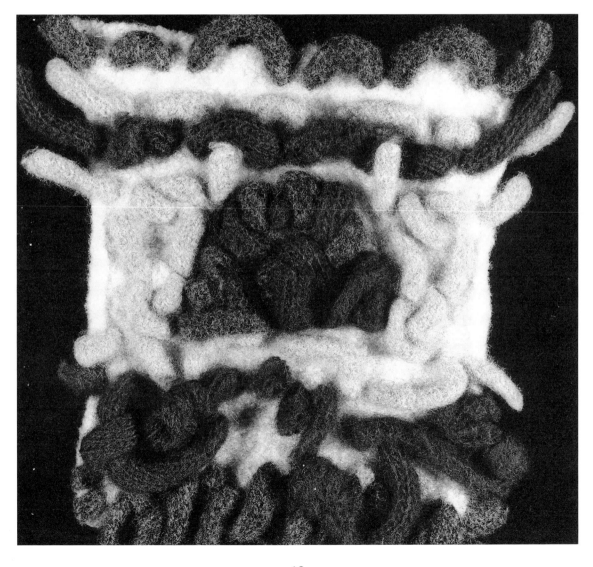

Introduction

There are a number of technical consider-ations when approaching felting with machine-knitted fabric.

1 The type and weight of yarn you use

a *Knitted fabric made only of wool* Al-though you may decide to use only wool fibres to make the knitted fabric that you will subsequently felt, you may decide that several different types of wool will provide a more interesting result. Lamb's wool felts to a different degree and at a different rate from, for instance, Shetland wool. If these two fibres are combined in a stitch construction your result will be quite different from a plain stocking stitch fabric made with only one type of wool. You may also decide to felt wools of a different thickness or compo-sition, such as lamb's wool and mohair or alpaca.

b *Knitted fabric made by mixing wool with other fibres* If you mix a yarn that will felt with a yarn that does not felt you will get a whole variety of interesting textural results.

2 The stitch size

The size of the stitch directly affects the ability of a yarn to form a thick matted fabric. The effect of the stitch size is also interdependent on the thickness of the fibre used.

3 Single-bed or double-bed fabric

This can affect the thickness of the final result but it is not always true that a double-bed fabric is twice as thick as a single-bed fabric. Depending on the thickness of the yarn and the size of the stitch used to construct the fabric, a single-bed fabric might easily be thicker than a double-bed fabric knitted in the same yarn.

4 Stitch type

Stocking stitch, Fair Isle, tuck, slip, weave, lace, plaiting, thread lace – there are many different stitch constructions which can lead to interesting and unexpected results, whether you are mixing colours, types of fibres or thicknesses of fibres.

All of these factors will affect the kind of fabric you produce and certainly you will have to take very careful precautions as to exactly how you carry out your felting depending on what end results you expect to achieve. You will also have to consider your garment design and the construction details, because these will affect the decisions you take about what kind of fabric you need to produce.

You will have to do a lot of sampling – that is, knitting a number of swatches in order to try out different variations, before you decide on the fabric you want to use for your garment. This is really very important, because no pattern can predict accurately how a particular yarn or stitch construction will react with your washing machine. You will have to determine for yourself what kind of fabric and what stitch pattern you want to produce. You will also have to design the garment in which you will use this fabric.

Type and Weight of Yarn

will give a wonderful variety of effects depending on the proportion of wool to non-felting fibres. You can also combine different types or qualities of wool which felt at different rates to achieve a variety of effects in a single fabric.

First of all, when you decide to felt wool that has simply been knitted up in stocking stitch, you will have to consider whether the yarn is thin or thick. The thicker the yarn the bigger your stitch size will have to be. Also, some yarns felt more easily than others, and you will need to make a sample using your particular yarn. It is often very difficult, when the yarn is wound on the cone, to tell what is the origin of the fibre. Even if you know, for example, that the yarn is a pure wool or a mixture of, say, 90% wool, 10% nylon, you must knit a sample to see how it will react in your washing machine. Sometimes a mix of wool and nylon or wool and silk will felt very well indeed, and sometimes not.

The other thing that can affect the ability of a yarn to felt well is the dye. If the same yarn is dyed several different colours, you may find that each of the dyed yarns felts to a different degree.

If you combine a yarn that will felt with a yarn that will not felt you can achieve a great variety of possibilities. You can combine the yarns in a variety of stitch constructions, of course, but even just knitting plain stocking stitch and changing the type of yarn you use,

Stitch Size

The next variable that will have an effect on your felting is the stitch size you use. Your choice of stitch size will depend on two things: the thickness of your yarn, and the effect you wish to achieve. The larger the stitch size you use, the thicker and denser your felt will be. You can knit with a very fine yarn and use a small stitch size, but you will find that your fabric will be lighter and have a very different handle from the fabric you make when you knit the same yarn at a much bigger stitch size. With a smaller stitch size you are less likely to lose the look of knitted fabric, and you will still be able to discern the individual stitches. With a bigger stitch size you will find your fabric is much heavier, denser, and stiffer. It will not drape, but it does have considerable 'body'. Such fabric is extremely warm and windproof. It is ideal for winter outer wear. The appearance of a 2-ply Shetland yarn (which comes with instructions specifying that it knits 'as a 4-ply yarn') seems to call out to be knitted on a standard gauge machine at approximately stitch size 7 or 8. When the yarn is supplied in oil this produces a fabric which resembles a string vest until it is washed, when it fluffs up nicely. However, if you try to felt this fabric you will find little change in its quality, feel and handle. The stitches seem still to be very apparent. This is because although the stitch size is big enough if you are just producing a knitted fabric, it is not

big enough to allow the yarn room enough to move about and 'entangle' in the washing machine to produce a satisfactory felted fabric. You may therefore find that with some yarns, you must knit them either on alternate needles on the standard gauge machine, or on a chunky gauge (9 mm) machine, in order to give the yarn enough room in the washing machine to produce a credible felted fabric.

If you are producing knitted fabric on a double bed with very fine yarn you may find knitting with a big stitch size is difficult. You will have to do some sample knitting to make sure that your stitches will not jump off the needles and to maintain an even fabric. The other consideration when knitting with very fine yarn on a Japanese or European machine with a ribber which requires weights to pull the stitches off the needles, is the difficulty of hanging the necessary weights. If you are knitting with a single strand of very fine yarn, and the yarn is very soft and delicate and pulls apart easily, you may find that it tears when casting on and hanging the casting-on comb on the first row. The way to get around this problem is to cast on with a stronger acrylic yarn. Knit several rows in this waste yarn. Knit 3 rows on the ribber only. Knit 1 row on both beds with the cast-on cord. Drop all the stitches off the ribber. Then, with the weights hanging on the waste yarn, cast on again with the fine wool. When you remove your work from the machine, you will be able to pull out the cast-on cord and remove the waste yarn. This is useful if you plan to use the cast-on edge of the felt. In fact if you decide to cut out the felted fabric to make your garment it is irrelevant whether the waste-yarn cast-on is present or not because you will just cut off and discard any unnecessary fabric. This type of fabric can be knitted in as loose a stitch as possible to make a lovely heavy, solid fabric with a firm handle and a great deal of character. It is particularly adaptable to roomy winter outer wear. Of course if you use a smaller stitch size, even on double-bed fabric you will achieve a thinner, more drapable felt.

Another difficult problem to deal with when knitting a fabric using a large stitch size is that the more room you give the yarn to move about in the washing machine, the easier it is for the fabric to felt to itself. This often happens when using a very fine, soft yarn and a very large stitch size. Sometimes it will occur at the outset when you are doing your sampling and only working with small swatches of 100 stitches by 100 rows. Sometimes you will find that the swatch is perfectly well behaved, but when you come to wash a much larger garment section, which can measure as much as 8 ft by 4 ft, it will emerge from the machine all screwed up and badly stuck to itself. When you try to pull it apart, you will only distort the felt and the piece will be unusable. This can happen whether the section has been knitted on the single or double bed. The main cause is using a too large stitch size for the type and thickness of yarn.

There is a way of dealing with the problem, and forewarned is definitely forearmed! You can use the same technique as is used to aid the felting of single-bed fabric. This is as follows. Firstly, steam-iron your knitting firmly and thoroughly after you have removed it from the knitting machine. Then lay a piece of loosely woven fabric made of cotton or synthetic yarn on the work surface. This piece of woven fabric must be wider and longer than your knitted piece. Lay the knitting down on top of the woven fabric, leaving about 60 cm (2 ft) of woven fabric uncovered at one end. Fold the extra woven fabric down over the end of the knitted piece and roll the whole thing up

fairly loosely. Fasten the roll securely so that it doesn't come apart in the washing machine. You can do this by fastening the woven fabric with safety pins, tying it with string, securing it with rubber bands, or tacking it together with a needle and thread. When you remove it from the first wash and unroll it, it will have begun to felt but it will by no means be processed evenly. Do not lose heart at this point. You will find that at least it has not stuck to itself. Now put it back into the washing machine under the same conditions, and run it through again. When it re-emerges for the second time you will find a perfect bit of felt!

Single-bed or Double-bed Fabric

When you are exploring the various possibilities of producing fabric, one of the most obvious choices will be whether to use a single or double-bed fabric construction.

If you choose to knit a single-bed fabric to felt you will have to deal with it in a very special way to avoid various pitfalls. One of the problems of dealing with a single-bed fabric is that it is susceptible to 'rolling'. That is, the side edges roll into the middle towards the purl side of the fabric, and the bottom and top of the fabric roll in towards the stocking-stitch side of the fabric. If you are not careful, you can find that your finished piece is much smaller than you had originally calculated, and also that the edges are rather thick and nasty and really unusable. One way to avoid this is first to steam-iron your knitted piece as flat as you can. Then fold your piece in half lengthwise or widthwise and using cotton thread sew it together loosely all around the edges until

Fig. 9 A piece of knitting placed on woven fabric

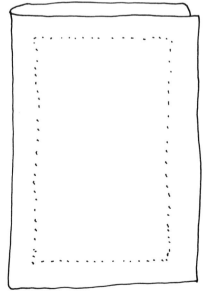

Fig. 10 Woven fabric folded over knitted piece

you have made a doubled-over pocket. Put this piece into the washing machine. You will find that it felts more evenly and there will not be a great difference between the shrinkage at the centre of the piece and at the edges. You will get less 'fluting' of the borders of the felted fabric. This means that more of the fabric is useful when you are planning and cutting out your garment.

However, if you have used a very big stitch size, this is not a good method to use because you may find that the two sides felt together and you will be unable to prise them apart without damaging them after the machine washing process. In this case, when the single-bed fabric uses such a big stitch size that you run the risk of the fabric sticking to itself during the felting process, you will have to resort to using woven fabric to protect your knitting from itself!

Lay a piece of woven fabric on your work surface. This piece must be both wider and longer than your knitted piece (Fig. 9). After carefully and firmly steam-ironing your knitting, lay it down onto the woven fabric. Take a second piece of woven fabric as big as the first piece and lay this on top of your knitting. Now, fold over the edges of the woven fabric (Fig. 10) and with a needle and thread, sew them into a small hem all around the knitted piece (Fig. 11). Then, using quite big stitches, sew through all three layers in straight lines 5 cm (2 in.) apart (Fig. 12), both up and down and across the whole piece. When you have finished lightly 'quilting' your fabric, fold it over or roll it loosely (Fig. 13) and put it into the washing machine. It will begin to form a satisfactory felt. You may feel that when you have removed it from the machine after the first wash, and removed all the stitching and woven fabric, that it is not felted enough. At this point you can just put it back into the washing machine and process it again under the same con-

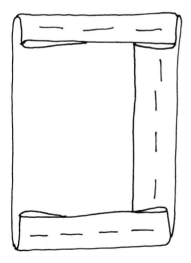

Fig. 11 Edges of fabric folded and sewn down

Fig. 12 Patchwork-like stitching to hold knitting in place

Fig. 13 The parcel folded up ready for felting

ditions but without sewing it into a protective casing. It will not stick to itself and should produce a most satisfactory fabric.

With any machine felting process, whether the fabric is knitted on the single or double-bed machine, some distortion takes place. The fabric felts and shrinks more in the centre than at the edges. This always results in slight fluting of the edge of the fabric, and it is important that you bear this in mind when planning how big a piece you will have to knit. You will have to make plenty of allowances for this sort of 'wastage' (fluting of the perimeters of the fabric). Otherwise you will find your piece of felted fabric is not big enough.

With double-bed fabric it is possible to create a variety of interesting fabrics by altering the way the 'backing' is knitted; that is, the way the second bed needles are programmed. All the needles can knit all the stitches on every row. This will result in a striped backing. If you decide to use a 'birds-eye' backing – that is, alternate needles knitting on alternate rows, resulting in a 1 × 1 backing which looks like a 1-stitch checked pattern – you will get a felt of a more uniform appearance on the reverse side of the fabric. Double-bed fabric does not roll up in the same way that single-bed fabric does, but if you use a very big stitch size to construct your knitted piece, it may still felt to itself in the washing machine. So just because you have used the double bed to construct your fabric, be careful when putting it in the washing machine, and remember to take proper precautions!

Stitch Type

It seems so obvious to say that if you vary your stitch pattern you will get a variety of fabrics but this is even more important when felting your knitting.

One of the most popular types of stitch pattern is *Fair Isle* or *jacquard* patterning. This involves using two different yarns on selected needles in the same row, and usually results in a marked visual image or pattern. If both yarns are wool of the same type and weight but only different in colour, the yarns will usually felt at a similar rate. You can use the Fair Isle pattern all over to get a flat, even effect in your felted fabric when knitting with two similar yarns. If, however, the yarns are different in weight, origin of fibre and composition, you can get quite a wide variety of results. Different patterns will also contribute to this variety.

The two elements that play the most important part in this are the proportion of one type of yarn to another, and the type of stitch pattern. If the proportion of the two different types of yarn is fairly even, you will get a very even type of felt with no discernible 'lumps and bumps'. If you use equal quantities of wool and synthetic fibre, you may not even achieve a felted effect at all!

If your stitch pattern is quite regular with both yarns distributed evenly across the fabric, you may find you get very little felting, no matter how hot you wash the fabric or how much you beat it about. Small areas of wool will felt quite well but if the woollen stitches are quite isolated from each other, do not expect miracles! If you use only wool in a Fair Isle design with a lot of very long floats, you can produce a really very interesting fabric because the floats will felt to themselves and pull up, producing a stocking stitch surface which gives the appearance of being moulded, almost quilted. If you are using two different types of wool, for example Shetland wool and lamb's wool, in the same Fair Isle fabric, even if they are the same colour you will get a fabric with surface interest because the two wools will felt at a different rate. Of course the differential felting effect is most pronounced if you combine wool with a synthetic yarn in Fair Isle knitting. In this case, if there is a fair proportion of wool, it will pull up markedly, making the other yarn, which does not shrink or intertwine, free to bubble up and produce a three-dimensional effect. With this fabric you may have to deal with the floats when it comes to constructing your garment. Garments made of felt that rely on long tangled floats to achieve their effects may have to be lined. Or, you may cut these floats and use them as a design feature.

When making double-bed jacquard fabric, your effect will rely on the knitting technique you employ far more than for single-bed jacquard fabric. If you only knit one type of yarn on the second bed, leaving the combination of yarns to be knitted selectively on the stitch patterning bed, you will produce marked three-dimensional felt. If you only knit with your woollen yarn on one bed, you will pull your knitting up into a much firmer, more stable fabric. Only knitting with the synthetic yarn on one bed will produce a lighter, less dense type of fabric that only felts a little.

Tuck stitch produces a fabric with a three-dimensional quality without felting. If you felt tuck-stitch fabric, you may find that you compress the yarn so much that the textural effect is almost lost altogether. Again, if you use a woollen yarn and a synthetic yarn in your stitch construction, you will find the proportion of one to the other will affect the result. Do not expect a small number of stitches knitted in woollen yarn, widely spaced in your fabric, to work miracles in pulling up large areas knitted in synthetic yarn. You may be very disappointed. But do not take my word for it. Make a small sample, because it is only through trial and error that you can discover your own methods of manipulating the felting process.

The effects that can be achieved with *slip stitch* are both surface texture and multicoloured jacquard. All comments made about single-bed jacquard in two colours apply also to multicoloured slip-stitch jacquard. However, a number of possibilities can be explored by knitting slip stitch to achieve a three-dimensional fabric in either woollen yarn only or woollen yarn alternated with synthetic yarn, then felting the knitted fabric.

Weaving can produce some very exciting results. If synthetic yarns are used in selected areas, these areas will not felt as well as areas where there is no weaving, resulting in a fabric which is quite exciting because it not only has different textural qualities, but it also appears to be quite three-dimensional.

None of these stitch variations requires any special techniques for producing the felted fabric from the knitted original. Even if you use various types of yarn, you can still put the knitted fabric into the washing machine and finish up with a felted fabric, because the temperature of the water does not have to be so high that it damages any synthetic yarn you include in your sample.

Of course, all these ideas are only suggestions and guidelines.

Garment Shapes

The type of garment shape you choose to make with your felted fabric will depend a great deal on the type of felt you are intending to produce. In general, felt is a fairly dense, thick, stiff fabric that does not fall or drape well. Its main characteristics or qualities are that it is windproof and warm, and forms a protective layer around the body. It is also water resistant (but not actually waterproof). Not the sort of fabric to use to make a bikini! Because it is so firm it is a good idea to keep the number of seams in your garment to a minimum. So the thicker your felt, the simpler the shape should be, with no darts. You will not have any problems with ravelling at the seams, but because the fabric is thick, seams tend not to lie flat, and if one seam crosses over another (for example under the arm where the sleeve joins the body of the garment), you can have a real problem with bulk. Of course, this does assume you are intending to produce a very dense fabric indeed.

There is no law that says that a whole garment has to be made in felt. You can combine felted fabric both with knitted fabric and with woven fabric to make up your garment. Felt can be used selectively to make the body or sleeves of a jacket. Or you can use felt to make the trimmings on a garment. You can have a knitted cardigan with a felted collar, front band, cuff, waistband, or yoke.

You can buy a paper pattern for a coat or jacket and adapt it for use with your felt. If the pieces of the pattern are bigger than the felt that you can produce on the full width of your needle bed, remember that you can always knit up two widths of fabric on your knitting machine and then sew them together with wool before felting them in your washing machine. If you take enough care in doing this, the seam will not be discernible from the right side of your fabric. When using a commercial pattern, try to choose one that is designed for a thick fabric. You will not have to make up all the facings, because then the garment would be much too thick. You could, for example, choose to edge the garment with a braid knitted on the machine using the same yarn you used for the felted fabric.

If you are drafting your own garment pattern based on your own measurements, you must be sure to allow quite a bit of ease to compensate for the bulk and density of the felt. Do not expect to achieve a garment with a great deal of sophisticated shaping detail. Keep the shapes simple and geometric if possible. Rely on the fabric pattern to give your garment interest.

One way of making a mock-up or toile of your pattern is to draft it out on paper, allowing plenty of ease, and then to cut out the shapes in fairly heavy-duty Vilene. Sew up your mock garment and try it on. You will very quickly see if it is big enough to go over your clothes, to fit comfortably and to allow you ease of movement. If it pulls anywhere it is quite easy to insert another strip of fabric to add fullness and ease. Once you have tested your shape you can transfer any alterations to your paper pattern. Then, when you come to cut out your felt, you can be sure that your garment will fit.

Another source of patterns for your felted garments could be to copy a jacket you already have that is comfortable and fits well. This was a technique first used by Kathy Duffee when drafting patterns for making a felted coat. Copy the shape of the pieces of your jacket or coat onto paper and cut them out in the thinnest quality of polyester wadding, which can be purchased by the metre from haberdashery stores or department stores. Then repeat the procedure described above to produce the Vilene garment. Here the thickness of the wadding will simulate the thickness of the felt. If the garment fits and is comfortable and flattering, you will have a very useful pattern.

Another technique for making felted garments is a little more hair-raising. You can knit great lengths of fabric and felt them in the washing machine. Then, when they emerge, you can drape them over yourself (or a model, or a friend) and cut and alter them until you achieve the effect you are looking for. There are no hard-and-fast rules for this, and you could be lucky or unlucky: you pay your money and you take your choice! The end result may well be quite extraordinarily exciting – much more so than if you tried to predict it! One positive aspect of playing this sort of game with felted fabric is that it *does not unravel*. This means that any cuts you make are 'safe' cuts, and you do not need to worry about finishing them off. You have far more room for manoeuvre than if you were working with either woven or knitted fabric. Remember also that after it has been constructed felted fabric can still be altered. With the use of steam and heat (a hot steam iron) you can shape, pull, widen, lengthen and generally distort felted fabric to manoeuvre it into any form you like. The only thing you cannot do is to make the fabric shrink after it has been felted – but you can cut it!

Construction Techniques

In making up your felted garments you must remember that your techniques must take into account the special qualities of the fabric: first, it is very thick; second, it does not ravel; and third, it can be moulded with heat and steam.

Seams do not always lie flat and care should be taken to minimize the bulk of these seams. One way of constructing your garment is to sew the sections together on the sewing machine in the ordinary way, pinning them so that the right sides are together, and then sewing them. When you have done that, there are several ways of making your seams lie flat.

- You can sew both seam allowances down flat on either side of the seam, and this will give you two lines of decorative top stitching on the right side of the garment.

- You can trim back one of the seam allowances and press the other seam allowance flat over this one and sew it down, catching the narrower seam allowance underneath. This will give you one decorative line of stitching near the seam on the right side of the garment.

- You can encase the seam in a knitted braid which you can fold over the seam allowances and sew on with the seam (Photo 1). The braid could be made on your knitting machine using the same yarn that was used to make the felted fabric. Or you can sew the seam together in the usual way, press it flat and then sew your braid down on top of the flat seam, hiding the seam edges. This will give you two decorative top stitching lines on the right side of your garment.

All these seam finishes can be executed on the inside of the garment. You can also make seams on the outside of the garment. The advantage of doing this is that you may decide the finished effect is nicer on the inside even though making the garment reversible is not particularly important.

If you make up your garment with the seams on the right side, you can make a felled seam by trimming back one of the seam allowances, folding the wider seam allowance over and pressing it down firmly over the narrower one with a hot steam iron, then sew it down. This makes quite a professional-looking finish but cannot be achieved successfully if your felted fabric is very thick.

Another method of dealing with a 'right-sided seam' is to press it open, as flat as possible, with a hot steam iron. Then sew down a braid which was made on the knitting machine outside both edges of the seam allowance so that they are covered completely. The fabric you sew down over your seam could be a braid knitted on the machine as either a single-bed or double-bed fabric. You could knit the braid with the same yarn used to make the felt, or with a contrasting yarn, or you could even use a strip of woven fabric cut on the bias, with the edges folded in and sewn down as a design feature. You might use this technique if you were making a coordinated outfit where the felted item was designed to be worn with another garment made of woven fabric, such as a jacket and skirt. Or you

1. *Knitted braid used as an edging and to cover seams*

could combine two types of fabric in one garment. The body might be felted and the collar, cuffs and hem might be made of woven fabric. Then you could use a braid made of bias-cut fabric to cover the felt seams (Fig. 14).

When dealing with the edges of your garment, you can hem them as you would any fabric garment, or you could just trim them back to a pattern line. Remember – the fabric does not ravel! It is a good idea to use an iron-on type of Vilene behind any felt that has been finished with a cut edge, to give the fabric added strength and to act as a kind of backing. You can also turn your edges in and line the garment with a fine plain or patterned polyester fabric, cotton or silk. Another method of 'finishing off' your garment is to edge the whole item with a braid which is easily made on the knitting machine. This will give a firm finished matching edge to your hem or cuff.

Your garments may require fastenings if you are wearing them as outer garments. You can make ordinary buttonholes in the usual way on a sewing machine and they can be strengthened by running a cord underneath the sewing machine foot when you are sewing the zigzag edge of the buttonhole (Photo 2). (Your sewing machine manual should give you information on how to do this.) You can also make a bound buttonhole using the same method as you would for a garment made in woven fabric.

If you are finishing the edges of your garment by sewing on machine-knitted braid, you can use the same braid to make fastenings, from elaborate frog fastenings for buttons, to simple loops at the front edge of the garment.

Zips are quite easy to insert, as they can be put straight under the two edges and sewn down without any need for elaborate facings or turnings. It is important to place a zip

Fig. 14 *The main part of the garment is made of felt, the collar and cuffs (added on) made of woven material*

carefully, so tack the zipper in by hand first before sewing it more firmly either by hand or by machine.

The thickness of felt is an advantage when it comes to other types of fastenings, as you can carefully hand sew hooks and eyes, large poppers or snaps and they will not be seen on the right side of the garment.

Pockets do not have to be faced either. You can place patch pockets on your garment wherever you want them and simply sew them down without worrying about the edges. You may wish to turn over the open end and sew it to the pocket to strengthen the part that gets the most wear.

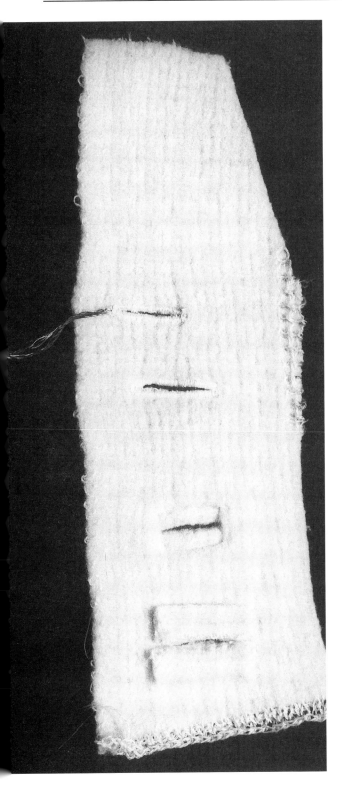

2. *Bound buttonholes, sewing machine buttonhole, reinforced sewing machine buttonhole*

The Samples 1

The first example of felt made in a washing machine is a hat which was made not using knitted fabric at all but using topps or dyed carded fleece. These topps have been layered carefully, the first layer facing in one direction and the next layer placed at right-angles to the first. Six layers were built up in this way and the whole thing was finished off using a combination of dyed wool topps and dyed unspun silk fibres. It was constructed approximately 50% bigger than the expected final result. The whole item was folded inside a length of fine woven fabric and sewn up very carefully. It was then put into a washing machine for the felting process. This technique was developed by Eva Kuniczak.

If you take the same yarn, and knit your fabric in varying stitch sizes, you will alter the type of felt you produce. The stitch size has far more influence over your final result than anything else you may try to do with your fabric, including boiling it!

Using a fine pure lamb's wool yarn (approximately 2/15–2/20), these swatches of 100 stitches by 100 rows were knitted at tensions 2, 4, 6 and 8 (Photo 3). The biggest swatch was also knitted at tension 8 but using Shetland wool. The swatches do vary in size as you would expect, but the biggest

difference is in 'handle' or 'feel' – they feel and behave quite differently! The swatch using the smallest stitch size is thinner and softer. It has a better draping quality and therefore can be used in finer garments. The stitches are still visible and there is no doubt as to the origin of the fabric. You could still use a cut-and-sew technique to construct the garment, and the fabric would not ravel as readily as it would if it was knitting that had not been felted. It could be used for example as a yoke in conjunction with knitted fabric, to make a top or dress. As the stitch size gets bigger, the felt becomes firmer and thicker and the appearance of the individual stitches begins to disappear. When you reach the swatch knitted at tension 8, the felt is quite firm and almost twice the thickness of the swatch knitted at tension 2.

Any garment made in this fabric would almost stand up in the corner on its own. This type of fabric does make a lovely coat or jacket but when designing the garment you must remember to keep seams and shaping to a minimum. Collars, cuffs and the edges of garments, where stiffened fabric is essential, would be ideal for using this type of felt. It could also be used to make very strong, attractive and serviceable bags, either large for carrying shopping, or small to use as a handbag. It would also be ideal for small items that need to be firm, such as spectacle cases.

Here are two comparative samples which have been hand-knitted in a complicated pattern in Shetland wool (Photo 4). One is felted and the other is not. The yarn used to knit these samples was doubled to make it thicker and therefore easier and quicker to knit. The knitted fabric produced was quite close in texture. One sample was put in the washing machine under the same conditions as were used to produce the other felt samples. Although the result was a slight

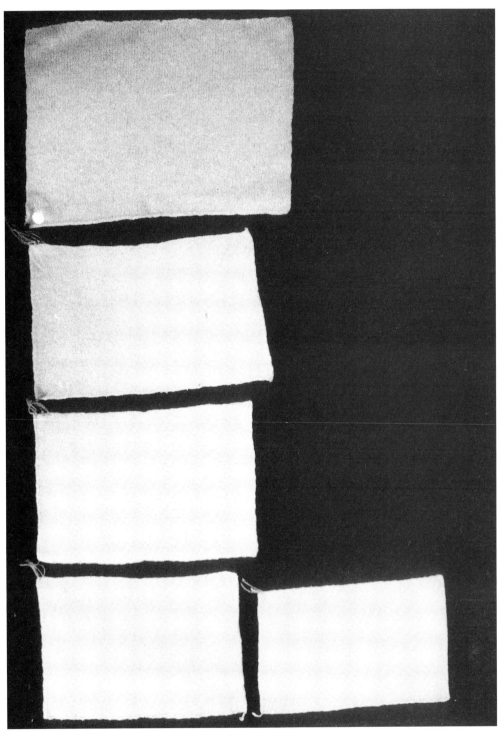

3. (samples from the bottom clockwise) Lambswool: stitch size 2, stitch size 4, stitch size 6, stitch size 8.
Shetland wool: stitch size 8

4. Hand knitting samples. The top one is felted

thickening, intermeshing and shrinking together of fibres, the process did not produce a felted fabric. Therefore, when the knitting itself is quite closely textured, the felting process is inhibited. Whether the fabric is produced by hand or by machine is irrelevant – it is stitch size that counts.

However, when a different stitch size is used in the same piece of knitting, it is very difficult to see the effect of this variation. In a swatch using the same yarn that was used to make the comparative stitch size swatches, I made a swatch 100 stitches wide and 110 rows long. I knitted 10 rows at tension 10 and 20 rows at tension 2 and the difference is hardly discernible. You can just see the stitches in the section knitted at tension 2,

6. Sample in photo 5 felted

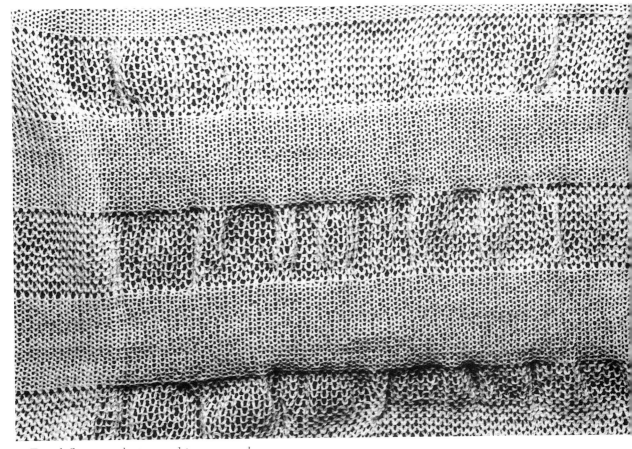

5. Two different stitch sizes used in one sample

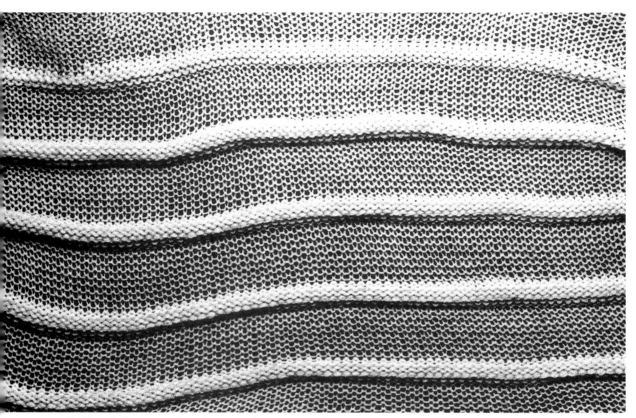

7. Two different weights of yarn used in one sample

8. Sample in photo 7 felted

but there is not enough of a difference to make this variation practical when producing felted fabric for a garment (Photos 5–6).

If you change the yarn you do create quite an interesting fabric. On this next sample (100 stitches and 110 rows), the same yarn and the same tension were used. The difference was that on some rows the yarn was plied-up; that is, five strands were knitted together as one strand (Photo 7). So 4 rows were knitted using one strand of yarn and 6 rows were knitted using five strands of the same yarn. We can see that the rows knitted with one strand felted very nicely forming a uniform matt fabric, but the rows using five strands of yarn did not felt at all and stand out in high relief (Photo 8). The appearance

of the individual stitches is quite distinct. This feature could be used quite effectively almost anywhere in a garment, giving a three-dimensional texture to an otherwise flat piece of fabric. The most obvious place to use this feature might be at the edges of the garment – hem, collar, etc. But it could be used to equal effect at the shoulders or vertically up the centre of a sleeve or a bodice.

We can also mix types of wool in the same fabric. Two different types of wool do not felt to the same degree, and in this swatch the stripes were knitted alternately with lamb's wool and Shetland wool using the same stitch size. The lamb's wool produced an even, homogeneous fabric, but the Shetland

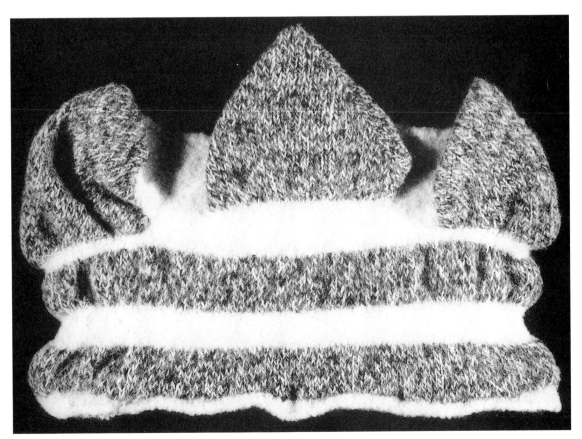

9. A sample using Shetland wool and lambswool

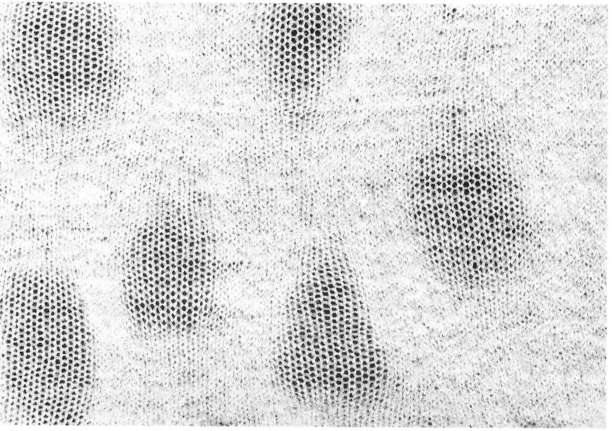

10 A sample felted after ironing on small pieces of plastic

wool hardly felted at all and bubbled up slightly, being pulled in by the shrinkage of the lamb's wool. The Shetland stitches are still discernible (Photo 9). The Shetland yarn was also used in the short-rowed areas which flute and gather, forming softer areas in the firmer lamb's wool felt. This feature could be used around a neckline to create a softening effect.

You can also prevent the felting process from taking place in some areas by blocking-off the knitted fabric before you put it into the washing machine. One way of doing this is to iron cut-up sections of plastic bags onto both sides of the knitted fabric before placing the sample into the washing machine. (Protect the iron and the ironing

board with pieces of non-stick silicone kitchen paper.) After the felting process has been completed, the plastic can be peeled off leaving an interesting bubbled surface which could be embellished later with fabric paint or embroidery. This fabric was knitted at tension 6, so it felted quite well, giving an intriguing contrast between the felted and non-felted areas (Photo 10).

Another way of stopping the felting process is to take a leaf out of the tie-dyer's book. Tie up small sections of your knitted fabric very tightly with string or non-felting yarn before putting it into the washing machine (Photo 11). Then, when it comes out, remove the string to leave little pimples of plain knitting in the felted fabric (Photo 12).

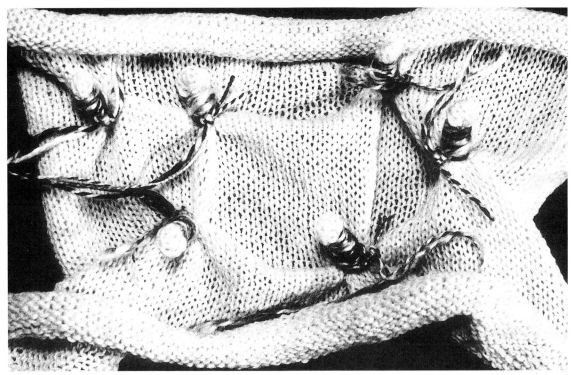

11. A knitted sample tied before felting

12. Sample in photo 11 felted

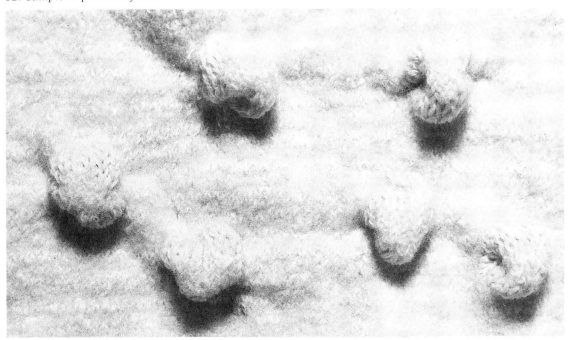

The Samples 2

You can also produce quite an interesting fabric by simply combining, in plain knitting, a yarn that felts with one that does not felt. If you knit strips of wool with cotton, the cotton will not felt and you will be able to see the individual stitches. The effect of combining two different yarns is also to give your fabric a different 'handle' or 'feel'. It can 'lighten' the fabric so that it can be used for a different type of garment. It could be used for a jumper, or even a shirt.

Combining lambswool with a fine acrylic which you knit at the same tension will produce a very light and floaty sort of fabric which could even be used to make a dressy garment for evening wear. It is quite interesting to use the contrast between rows of firm,

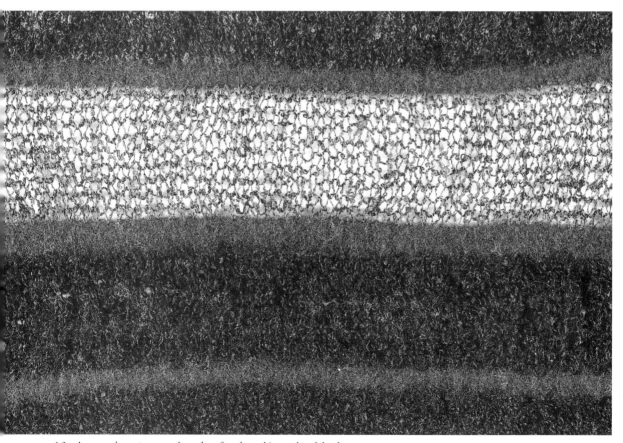

13. A sample using wool and a fine bouclé acrylic felted

thick felt with the transparent qualities of a fabric made of a fine thin acrylic yarn knitted with a large stitch size. This gives the felt a soft, fuzzy, almost brushed appearance. The felting of the wool also produces a gathering effect on the acrylic which could be quite attractive in sleeves or a full skirt or as an inset in a cape (Photo 13).

You can use the same stitch size on the whole piece of knitting even though you vary the yarn, but remember that once the piece has been felted, the sections knitted in lamb's wool will contract and shrink owing to the felting process, while the other yarn will remain unchanged (Photo 14). This will affect the width of your fabric and while the felt will not ravel back if you cut and sew it,

the other yarn may well do so. You will need to pay particular attention to the construction methods used in this type of garments, and even more so to the finishing techniques you decide to use.

If you have some decorative acrylic yarn, you may knit this in occasional single rows to produce a fabric where the variation in colour and texture of the acrylic yarn is shown off to advantage by the smooth, even, matt finish of the felted wool (Photo 15). Interesting yarns of this type, used sparingly, can be a really beautiful design feature of the fabric. However, if they are used on their own or in too large a proportion with another yarn and are therefore 'over-exposed', they often lose their effectiveness

14. A sample using cotton slub and wool felted

15. A sample using wool and a decorative textured yarn felted

and just finish up looking messy and untidy.

Interesting colour effects can be achieved by mixing wools of different colours in the same stocking-stitch fabric. There are several ways of mixing colours in your knitting. You can simply ply-up the yarns, knitting two yarns together as if they were one. If the two yarns are different colours you will get a random striped effect in your knitting and consequently in your felted fabric. Your felted sample using two strands will of course be much thicker than if you only use one strand. To increase the feltability of your knitting you will also have to increase the stitch size by a considerable amount. The sample shown was 100 stitches by 100 rows knitted on stitch size 6, but

although the fabric has thickened and felted somewhat, the stitches are still discernible and the stitch size would have to be much increased in order to convert the knitted fabric into truly felted fabric (Photo 16).

Another method of mixing coloured yarns is to knit the fabric in Fair Isle using a very simple one-by-one pattern. Although the sample shown was 100 stitches by 100 rows using the same yarn and the same tension (6), the finished size of the sample is quite different from the one where the yarns were merely plied-up (Photo 16). The first sample measures 24.5 cm wide and approximately 16 cm long ($9\frac{1}{2} \times 6\frac{1}{4}$ in.). The Fair Isle sample on the other hand is 15 cm wide and 16 cm long ($6 \times 6\frac{1}{4}$ in.). In this sample, the

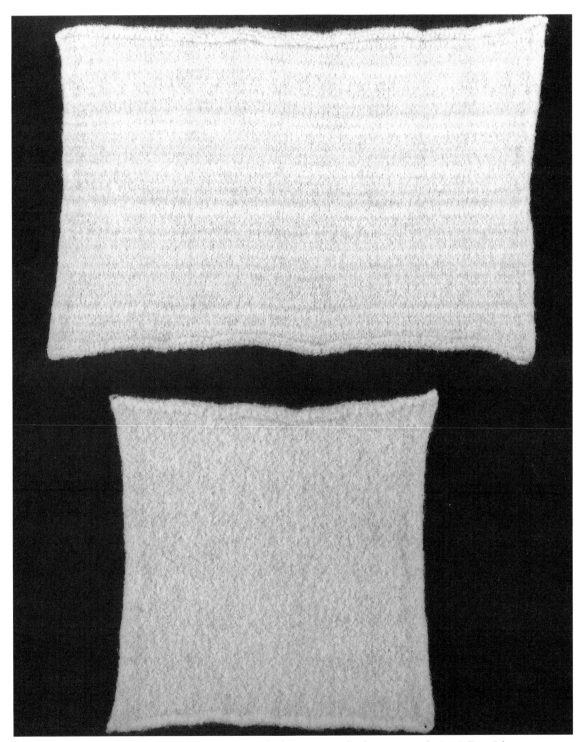

16. *The top sample shows two colours plied-up, the bottom sample shows a simple 1 × 1 Fair Isle pattern using the same two yarns*

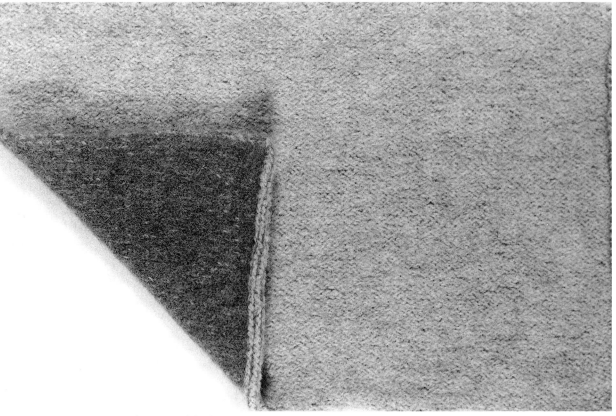

17. A sample of plaiting felted

Fig. 15 (Below) Plaited knitting used for collar and cuffs

stitches have disappeared and the fabric is very slightly thicker, but not noticeably so. The colour dispersal is more even and there is no evidence of any striping.

You can also use two different yarns to create a double-sided effect by plaiting your knitting (Photo 17). The swatch showing the plaiting effect was also 100 stitches by 100 rows knitted at tension 6, and the measurements are almost the same as the swatch using the two yarns plied-up. The feel, however, is quite different. This swatch is thinner, softer and more drapable. This technique would be quite effective if used in a jacket or top where the collar, reveres and cuffs folded back showing the 'wrong' side of the fabric, making a feature of the two-coloured double-sided fabric (Fig. 15).

Hand-manipulated Techniques on the Machine

Some hand-manipulated techniques used on the knitting machine to produce interesting pattern variation in knitted fabric can also affect the final appearance of the felted fabric.

Adding on 'bits and pieces' of knitting as you knit your fabric can produce flaps in a variety of colours and shapes which will give the fabric a three-dimensional aspect. These will not in fact felt with the background fabric if they are left loose when the knitting is put into the washing machine. In the sample, the layers were produced by picking up sections that had been scrapped off onto waste yarn or removed from the machine with the garter bar (Photo 18). The swatch was knitted at tension 4 over 50 needles. The first section, at the bottom, was knitted for 40 rows and then removed from the machine. The second section was then cast on and 20 rows were knitted. The first section was picked up onto the needles and a

further 20 rows were knitted on the second section, which was then removed again from the machine. The process was repeated to produce the third section, which was finally cast off. The piece was felted in the washing machine and the three sections remained totally separate. After finishing by placing in the tumble dryer for 10 minutes, the felt was laid out flat to dry. As the three sections did not felt together, they could be trimmed and decorated separately afterwards. A decorative edge was cut on the sections. To achieve a further decorative cut-out effect, you could also cut carefully shaped holes in each of the layers to create a window, through which you could see the fabric underneath.

Another decorative effect achieved by hand manipulation when producing fabric on the knitting machine is to lay-in previously knitted tubes as you are knitting your fabric (Photo 19). The tubes or strips, knitted in lamb's wool, will also felt while you are felting the knitted fabric. You must prepare your strips and plan out your pattern before you begin knitting the fabric. You can knit strips over 4–8 needles as long as you like before you begin. Then as you knit, remove a group of 2–3 stitches from the needles (Photo 20). Place the strip of knitting behind the stitches and then replace them on the needles. This will 'catch-in' your strips. You can use one strip at a time or you can use several. You can tie knots in them or you can tie them together, twine them, braid them, cross them, cut them and even thread beads on them. They will felt in the washing machine and the knitted fabric will felt around them and hold them quite fast. On one side of the fabric (the purl side) you can produce quite a lovely three-dimensional raised effect and on the reverse side (the stocking-stitch side) you get lovely little knobs where the strip shows up.

You can also produce a three-dimensional

18. *A sample of three different yarns knitted in sequence and cut after felting*

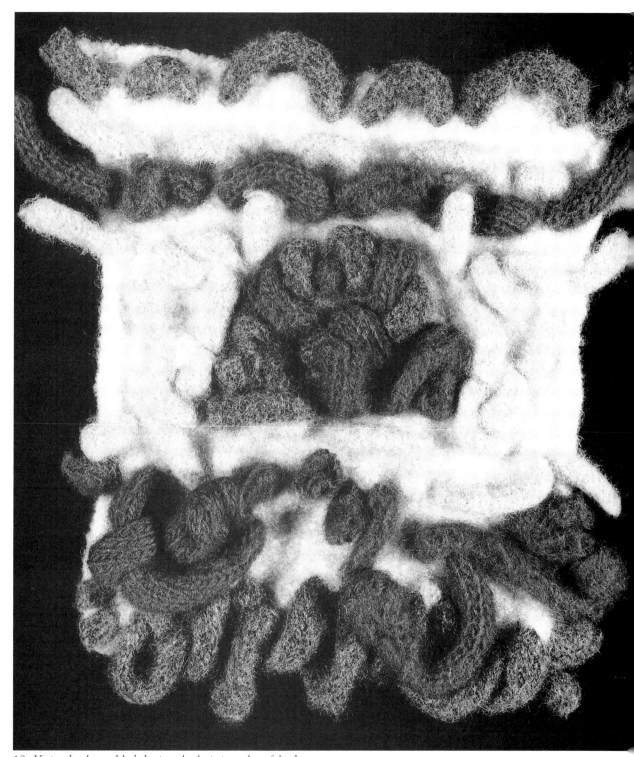

19. Knitted tubes added during the knitting, then felted

20. *Adding tubes while knitting*

21. Bobbles with cut floats felted

effect and make the colour of the felted fabric more exciting by knitting bobbles with floats in between each one along one row (Photo 21). You can do this by knitting 4 stitches and then leaving 20 stitches consecutively along the row. This sequence will enable you to punch a card out to select the needles. However, you can also select them by hand to upper working position (UWP). Then set the pattern dial or buttons on your machine to partial, slip or empty. If you decide to knit the bobbles further apart or to use a different number, you will not be able to use the automatic patterning system unless you have an electronic knitting machine, so the needle selection for knitting the bobbles will have to be by hand. For a Pfaff/Passap machine you need to use your pushers to select the needles you require for your bobbles and then set the cam box to BX

or LX to achieve the same result on single-bed knitting.

The first row of the bobbles can be picked up after knitting them to close them up. The floats are then cut and pulled through to the right side before the fabric is felted. The bobbles were knitted every 20 rows and their position was staggered every time they were repeated. The number of rows used to knit the bobbles was also 20. The whole sample was knitted at tension 4. In order to stagger them on an electronic knitting machine, the first needle position needs to be altered every time another set of bobbles are knitted. In this sample, the stitches on the four needles used for the bobbles were transferred to the gate-pegs before the bobbles were knitted. This meant that when they were finished, the stitches could be returned to the needles and there would be no need to pick up the bobble stitches. The bobbles would also be more rounded in appearance when they were finished. As you can see from the sample, some of the wool felted more closely and the appearance of the felted floats differs from bobble to bobble.

Making holes in the knitted fabric is also a feature that can be used in felting. You can leave needles in non-working position to create ladders and then, when your fabric has been felted, you can use these ladders to thread decorative braid or rick-rack through. You must remember that the effect of felting will be to close up the holes of the ladders. So you must be sure to make these

22. *Decorative braid added after felting*

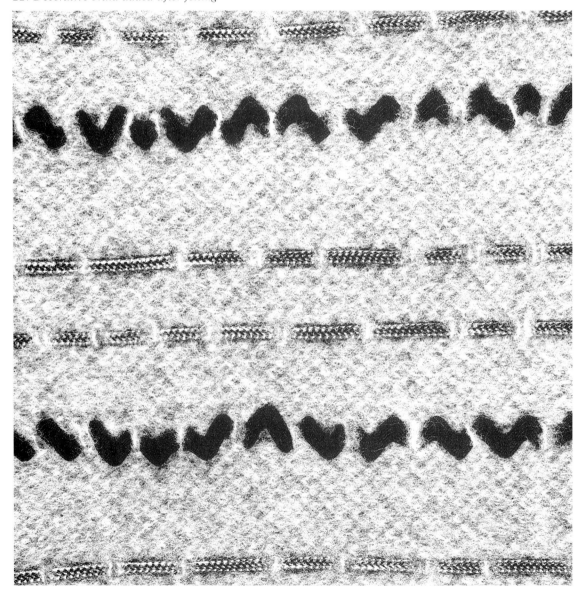

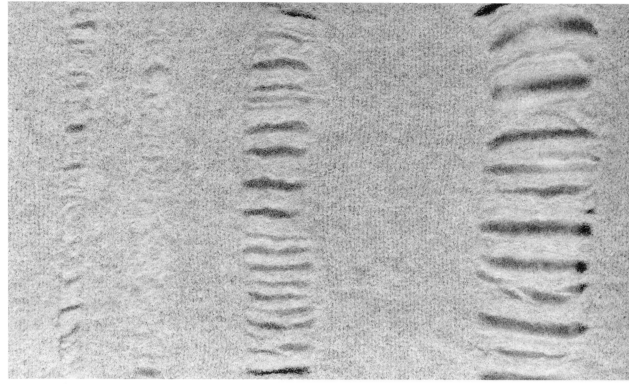

23. Knitted fabric, laddered then felted

'ladders' really quite big; that is, leave quite a large number of needles in non-working position.

On the sample, needles were not left in non-working position but the whole sample was knitted up in the Fair Isle technique on 100 stitches and 100 rows at tension 4. Then before casting off, stitches were dropped off *selected needles only* and run back to the cast-on edge while the remaining stitches were cast off. This left a wider ladder than that which would have resulted if the same needles had been put to non-working position before the sample was knitted. After felting, decorative trims were threaded through the 'ladders' (Photo 22).

If stitches are dropped off a larger group of needles (e.g.10) and the knitting is unravelled or run back to the cast-on edge, a wider ladder results. The floats of yarn felt-

up to produce a very interesting and attractive effect which is quite different from the fringing that would occur if the knitted fabric had not been felted. This unusual see-through visual effect can be put to good use depending on what is behind these windows. You can, by felting, attach this piece of knitting to another piece of knitted fabric in another colour underneath and then put them both in the washing machine and allow them to felt together. The sample shown was knitted over 100 stitches and 100 rows at tension 4 (Photo 23). The underneath sample, in another colour, was knitted on the same number of stitches and rows using the same tension but, because it was not unravelled, it is much narrower. The two samples felted together at one side, but remained separate and distinct at the opposite side.

Knitting separate strips of different col-

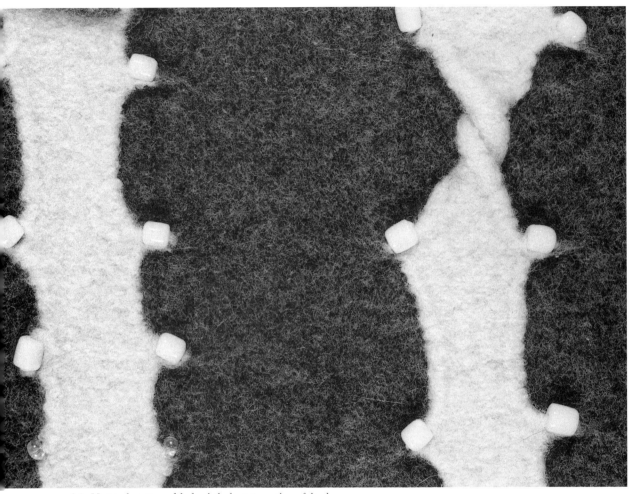

24. *Knitted strips added while knitting, then felted*

oured woollen yarn in preparation for 'adding' them onto your knitted fabric is an interesting way of adding not only colour and texture but also pattern to your felt. The strips can be in a different colour, type of yarn, and stitch size. One way of adding them on is to pick up the edge stitches from the strip as you knit and place these stitches onto your working needles. You can manipulate the strip before you pick it up onto your knitting by tying, binding, wrapping, or twisting it. In the sample illustrated the edges of the strip (which was knitted at tension 6) were picked up onto the sample

which was knitted at tension 4 (Photo 24). Beads were picked up at the same time. The strip was also twisted at one point before it was picked up. In some places the two pieces of knitting felted together and in other places they did not. This does not really matter a great deal in this case as the edge was firmly anchored to the background. The swatch was knitted on 100 stitches and over 100 rows.

Adding beads before felting the fabric is a very good way of incorporating them into your felt. When you want to pick up very big beads, you must be sure that the carriage

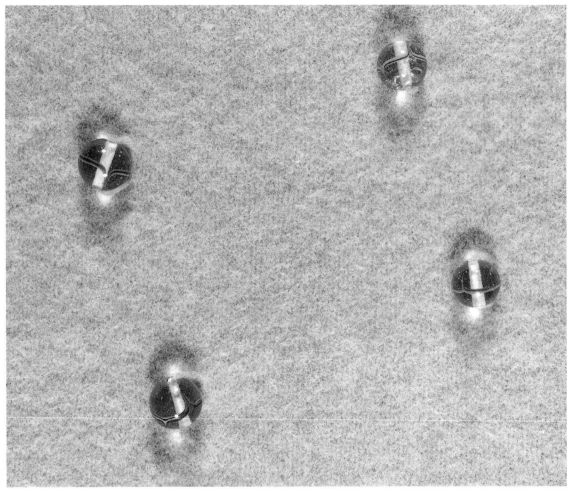

25. *Large beads added while knitting, then felted*

is able to move freely across the needle bed after the beads have been picked up. The sample illustrated was knitted over 100 stitches and 120 rows at tension 4 (Photo 25). To pick up large beads, you transfer 1 stitch where you want the bead to go. Leave the empty needle in working position. Knit 6 rows. Drop the stitch above the hole and run it back to the hole. Put the bead onto your crochet hook and put the hook behind the floats. Place the bead (behind the floats) on the first float after the transferred stitch by pulling it through the bead with the crochet hook. Then place this float onto the empty

needle. Knit 2 rows and push the bead through to the stocking-stitch side of the knitted fabric. After the fabric has been felted in the washing machine the bead will be securely and invisibly attached.

A good way of attaching very small beads is to thread them onto sewing cotton (Photo 26). The holes are too small for a crochet hook to go through them so you will not be able to pick them up onto your knitted fabric. In the sample illustrated, which was knitted on 100 stitches and 100 rows at tension 4, the beads were so small I had difficulty even threading them onto sewing

26. *Small beads added while knitting using the weaving technique, then felted*

cotton with a very fine needle. After preparing the sewing cotton with the beads threaded on, I selected alternate needles to holding position by hand. Then I wove the beaded sewing cotton, by hand, over and under the needles, making sure the beads would not foul the movement of the needles or the carriage. I then knitted 1 row with the sewing cotton hanging down very loosely. After the row had been completed, I pulled up the excess sewing cotton and this pulled up the beads. Even though the sewing cotton was in a contrasting colour, it disappeared completely after the knitting had been felted in the washing machine. The beads were incorporated into the fabric and it saved me the time it would have taken to attach each bead individually by hand afterwards. It also means that the beads are attached more securely, as they are held in place by the fabric itself.

These are a few suggestions as to how you might approach your knitting more creatively to produce an exciting and interesting felted fabric. You must make a lot of samples yourself to discover other exciting possibilities. Once you have decided how to produce your fabric, you will still have to decide how it will be used in the garment.

More Felting Techniques

Some of the special qualities of the felting technique can be used to push the boundaries of decoration a bit further. One of these qualities is the ability of one piece of knitted wool to 'stick' to another piece of knitted wool during the felting process. You can make two totally separate pieces of knitting and place one of them on top of the other before putting the whole lot through the felting process (i.e. into the washing machine) and the end result will be a single fabric. In this way you can decorate the whole surface of your fabric selectively so that patterned areas will be carefully placed where you want them and you will be able to

27. Knitted strips woven, tacked on to knitting, then felted

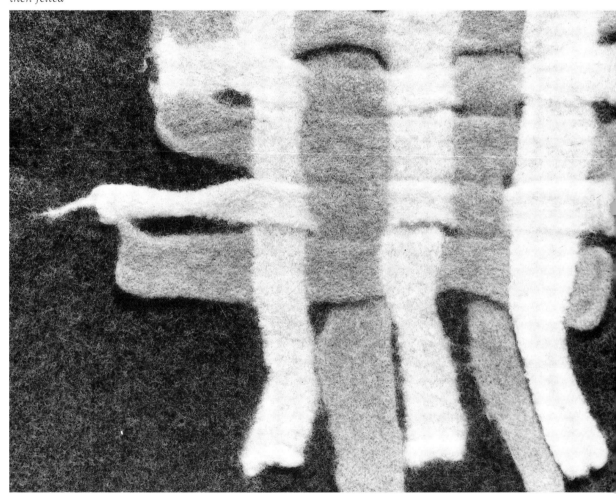

pre-plan these areas to coincide with the garment pattern.

We know that knitting, once felted, can be cut without fear that the fabric will fray or unravel. However, knitting can also be cut carefully *before* the felting process has taken place and then, after a period in the washing machine, it will felt and there will be no further changes (fraying or unravelling). If we take advantage of these two facts we can create some very interesting decorations.

In the first sample, the background was knitted at tension 6 over 100 stitches and 120 rows (Photo 27). Then two other pieces of knitting in other colours were produced. Each of these was 50 stitches and 100 rows at

28. Ravelled knitting tacked on to a knitted sample, then felted

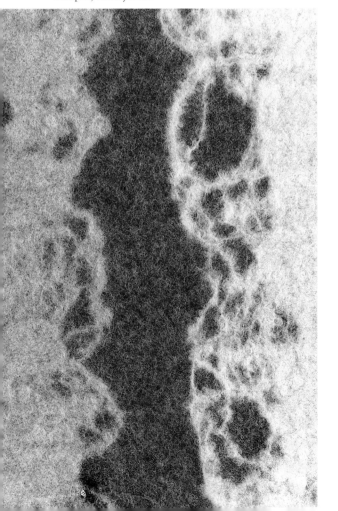

tension 4. The three pieces were then steam-ironed to flatten them out. The two smaller pieces were cut into strips and the strips were woven together. Then the woven strips were placed onto the big piece of knitting and the whole thing was tacked together carefully with sewing cotton. The piece of knitting complete with the woven section tacked on was then placed onto a large piece of cotton muslin which was folded over the top. The whole assembly was then rolled up so that no part of the knitting could touch itself. The roll was fastened firmly so that it did not come apart in the washing machine. It was placed in the machine and washed with Sansolaine (a mild detergent) at 30°C (86°F) on an ordinary half-wash with a plimsoll thrown in for good measure. Several other samples were included in the same wash. When it was removed from the machine, because it had been rolled up it was not evenly felted but, in the main, most of the woven strips had been amalgamated with the background. It was then put through the washing process again and the felting process was completed. So we can see that the ability of knitted fabric to felt to itself can be used to advantage to create some interesting three-dimensional effects, and this concept could certainly be taken much further with a little experimenting.

The same idea was used in the next sample (Photo 28). The background was knitted first on 100 stitches and 100 rows at tension 6. Then using an open cast-on, two more sections of knitted fabric were produced using different coloured yarns. These were done over 90 stitches and cast off after knitting 40 rows. The cast-on edge was then unravelled on purpose to create an open lace-like edge. The two sections were placed onto the background and tacked down with sewing cotton and the strands of unravelling were also carefully tacked in place. The

29. *Cut knitting and 'topps' tacked on to a knitted sample, then felted*

whole piece was then folded into muslin and rolled ready to place into the washing machine to be felted. It was treated in much the same way as the first sample and has resulted in a very interesting patterned fabric which is entirely homogeneous.

Dyed topps placed onto knitted fabric will also produce a homogeneous fabric when felted in the washing machine. You can almost 'draw' with strands of these dyed topps. They are pulled out and laid across the knitted fabric according to your own design. The design can be based on a drawing, collage or even a photograph that you find attractive or interesting. The topps can be used on their own, or you can add

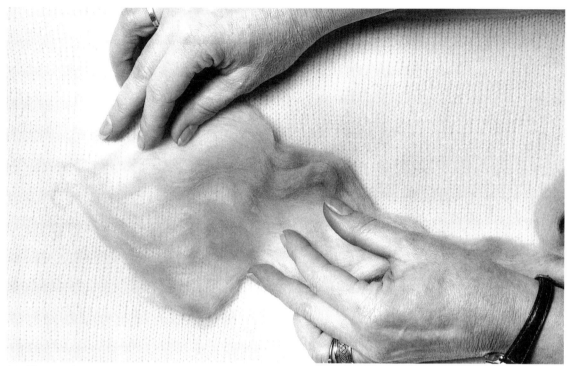

30. Placing the topps on the knitting

pieces of cut knitting (to create an appliqué effect), lengths of knitted tube, strands of woollen yarn or even cut-up pieces of woollen fabric. In fact, you can lay on top anything you think would be likely to felt in with (or stick to) your knitted fabric. A note of warning: tack all these bits down very carefully and thoroughly so that they will not move during the felting process. The sample comprises a background knitted over 100 stitches and 120 rows at tension 8 which was then cast off and steam ironed to flatten it in preparation for the application of decorations (Photo 29). Another piece was made over 90 stitches and 66 rows at tension 4. This piece was also steamed flat. It was then cut in half in a jagged way and the two sections were spread apart. One was tacked onto one edge of the background knitting, the other was tacked onto the opposite edge. The topps were then spread out across the

middle of the sample and tacked down by hand with sewing cotton (Photo 30). The whole swatch was then folded up in a piece of muslin so that no part of it touched another part of the knitting. The assembly was rolled up loosely but tacked together firmly so that it would not unroll in the washing machine. The roll was placed into the machine which had been filled with an 'ordinary' wash (socks, trousers, towels, etc.) and washed with detergent at 30°C (86°F) as normal. When the sample was removed from the machine the fibres had amalgamated but the finish was not sufficiently uniform to be satisfactory, so the sample was returned to the machine with another wash as before and the final result was then put into the tumble dryer for 10 minutes. It produced quite an acceptable fabric. This technique of surface decoration is certainly worth further exploration.

Decorative Techniques

The knitting machine can produce knitted fabric very quickly and efficiently and sometimes we think that our creative processes should allow the machine to do all the work for us. It is so good at it. But there are lots of alternatives for us to explore which do not necessarily rely totally on the knitting machine. We can combine machine-knitted

fabric with other techniques to produce interesting fabrics or interesting patterns on our fabrics. Do not be blinkered in your thinking or creative vision, but try to think laterally. What can be done if another skill or technique is used to create a pattern variation that no-one has ever thought of before?

When knitted fabric is felted in the washing machine, it not only changes its texture and composition – its style – but it also changes its *size*. It forms a matt fabric in which the fibres intertwine, and get closer together, so the area of the fabric decreases and it gets smaller. In other words, the fabric shrinks. If we appliqué a piece of fabric woven with a non-felting fibre onto the knitting before felting, the knitting will shrink and the woven appliqué will not. So it will gather up and create an interesting decorative effect. In this sample the knitted

31. Fabric appliquéd on to knitting, then felted

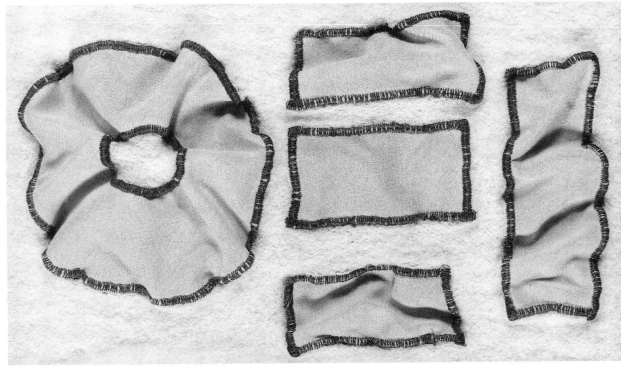

background was made over 100 stitches and 100 rows at tension 6 (Photo 31). It was cast off and steam-ironed to flatten it. The fabric was then machine appliquéd on top of the knitting. The fabric was carefully trimmed back to the stitching line on one side and the knitted fabric was cut away from behind it on the other side so that the appliquéd fabric has no backing behind it at all. This is important in achieving this effect. You could try appliquéing fabric on top of knitting but leaving the knitting behind to see what the effect might be. The knitting in this case is just a piece of plain stocking stitch. What would happen if the knitting background was done in a stitch pattern? The critical point to remember when experimenting with this technique is to keep the appliqué shapes as simple as possible. It is also important to use a fairly thin fabric which will not need ironing after it is washed. If the fabric is too thick or firm it will impede the felting process of the knitting. The shapes also need to be spaced out to allow the knitting in between them to felt properly. It is interesting to see how the felt in the centre of the circle has managed to gather up and pull in the fabric surrounding it. You could also use water-soluble embroidery fabric in a similar way to create an embroidered open-work effect on the knitting before you felt it.

The other feature of the shrinkage that occurs in the felting process is to 'grab' and hold anything that has been 'pushed' into it. In this sample, which was knitted over 100 stitches and 100 rows at tension 6, strips of torn fabric or tubes of knitting can be pushed into the felt using a rug-making tool (Photo 32). The knitting was stretched in an embroidery frame. The fabric was nicked at the selvage and then torn across to the opposite selvage, nicked again and torn again so that a very long strip of fabric was produced. This was threaded into the rug-

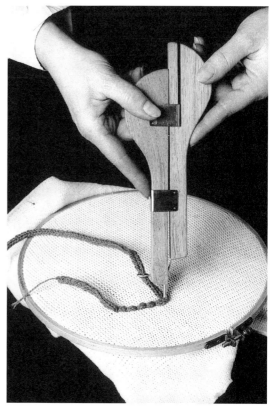

32. Using a rug punch tool

making device and was pushed through the knitted fabric from the back to form little loops on the front surface of the knitting. As the knitting was done in a fine strand of pure wool with a loose tension, it was quite easy to do. The sample was then felted in the washing machine. The knitting shrank and now holds the loops of fabric in place quite firmly (Photo 33). Again, variation could be achieved by making the knitted fabric patterned or using more decorative strips of fabric or ribbon for the surface decoration. The pattern produced could be quite lovely and free flowing, following the design lines of the garment. This technique of applying decorative areas made of strips could also be adapted to knitted cord. In this sample the background was knitted over 100 stitches and 100 rows using tension 6 (Photo 34). A

33. Strips of fabric punched into a knitted sample, then felted

34. Strips of cut knitting punched into a knitted sample, then felted

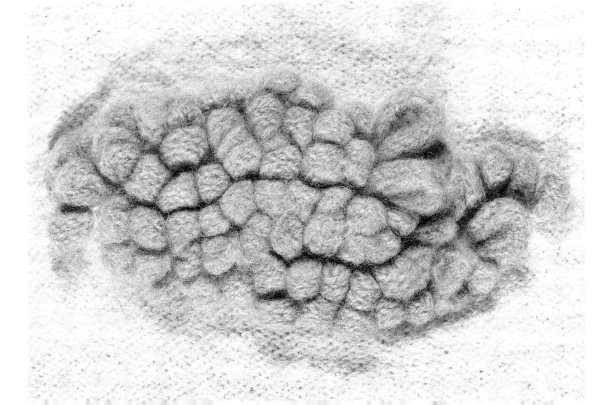

second piece of knitted fabric was produced in another colour knitted over 40 stitches and 100 rows at tension 6. The second piece was then cut into strips and threaded through the rug-making tool.

The knitting was stretched taut in an embroidery frame and the cut strips of knitting were pushed through the fabric to form a pattern on the other side. This sample was then felted and the decoration felted as well as the background. It has produced a soft textured three-dimensional effect which has quite a lot of body and is very firm and secure.

The amazing ability of cut knitting to felt smoothly and produce a finished fabric means it can be used to make a fabric of any width, and provides a way of creating a variation of surface pattern. One of the problems of machine felting machine knitting is that the width of the fabric is limited to the width of the needle bed and if the fabric shrinks width-wise a great deal during the felting process, this can be a further limitation on your garment design. However, it is possible to create a fabric of any width at all by connecting two strips or pieces of knitting before they are placed in the washing machine to be felted.

Another problem connected with the knitting machine is that if you are using the automatic patterning facilities or even just knitting in stripes, you will produce a fabric that is horizontally consistent. That is, the pattern, the colour and the stitch will be the same across the whole width of your knitting (unless you are using the intarsia technique, but this is not explored here). If the width of your knitting could be made up of several different sections joined together you would be able to escape this constriction and produce a felted fabric which you could vary in pattern and design across the width as well as in the length.

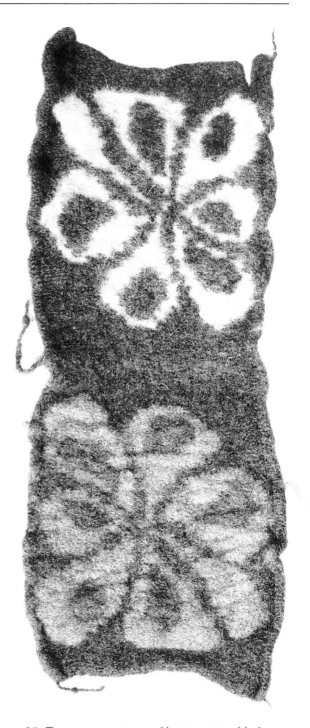

35. *Two separate pieces of knitting joined before felting*

There are several ways of joining two pieces of knitting. One is to knit the first strip and complete it. Remove it from the machine. As you are knitting the second strip, pick up a stitch at the edge of your first strip onto the end needle of your knitting on every other row. This may sound tedious but it does give an invisible join and when the knitted fabric has been through the washing machine and felted, it cannot be seen from the right side. This will enable you to produce a felted fabric of any width. As you can see from this sample, the two motifs are knitted in different colours (Photo 35). They were knitted separately using only one contrast colour at a time, but as the second one was being knitted, the first one was picked up at the edge. This seam could be seen until the fabric had been felted, and it is still not completely invisible.

Another way of joining the knitted strips

together is simply to join them with the wool that was used to knit them. This can be done by hooking both pieces back onto the knitting machine, knitting one row and casting off; it can be done by hand, using a sewing needle or a crochet hook; and it can be done on a linker. Any method is quite effective and acceptable.

In the first sample three strips were knitted over 40 stitches and 100 rows at tension 4 (Photo 36). The knitting was done using arbitrary striping of different coloured wools. The strips were then cut in half and reformed. They were linked together to form a single fabric on the linker and then put into the washing machine to be felted. They have produced a very nice light felted fabric with a pleasant handle and drape. The felt is not too thick and the seams are apparent on the wrong side but do not appear on the right side.

36. *Strips of striped, cut knitting joined, then felted*

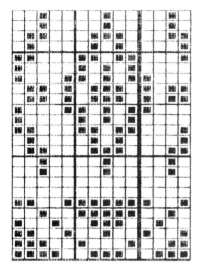

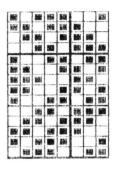

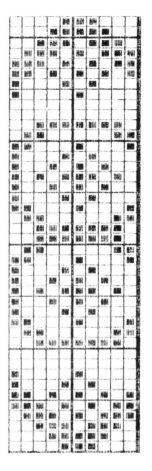

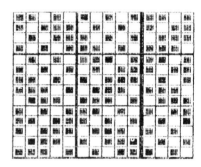

Figs. 16–19 Fair Isle stitch patterns

The second sample is thicker as a Fair Isle technique was used (Photo 37). Remember, knitting a Fair Isle fabric is like knitting two fabrics at the same time because two wools are running alongside by side. In this sample three different Fair Isle patterns were used but the yarn remained the same throughout (Figs. 16–19). Although the three swatches were also knitted over 40 stitches and 100 rows at tension 4, cut in half and reformed as in the previous swatch, this sample is thicker and firmer. It is also quite different in size. Both samples were measured after felting. The striped sample is 24 cm wide and 14 cm long ($9\frac{1}{2} \times 5\frac{1}{2}$ in.). The Fair Isle sample is 19.5 cm wide and 17.5 cm long ($7\frac{3}{4} \times 7$ in.)!

In the last sample I used more varied colours in the knitting. This swatch was produced using three different stitch patterns and using four different colours of yarn: dark grey, red, light blue and white (Photo 38). Three strips were knitted over 50 stitches and 120 rows at tension 4. The strips were all steam-ironed to help to flatten them out. Each strip was then cut in half and the whole fabric was re-formed. It was then linked on a linker. It produced a felt similar in weight and feel to the other sample that was knitted using the Fair Isle technique (Photo 39). Again the front surface seems quite homogeneous to look at and to feel. You can only see and feel the seams on the wrong side, and the fabric is not unduly stiff; suitable for a lightweight jacket or suit.

38. Strips of Fair Isle knitting cut and joined

39. Sample in photo 38 felted

37. Strips of Fair Isle knitting cut, joined, then felted

Once you know you can cut the knitting and re-form your fabric you can achieve all sorts of patchwork possibilities. You could also create a fabric wide enough and long enough to make an apparently 'seamless' garment: make up the garment *before* the felting took place rather than afterwards.

Fair Isle and Thread Lace

Sometimes experiments can be very exciting and sometimes they can be very disappointing indeed. Often an idea you might have seems wonderful and then when you have spent a great deal of time and effort in executing it, it falls like a damp squib, or even a soggy piece of felt, out of the washing machine and into your hand. This can happen when experimenting with Fair Isle and thread lace.

Fair Isle and thread lace are very closely related machine knitting techniques. In Fair Isle patterning some needles (selected according to a charted or punch card pattern) knit one colour of yarn while the remaining needles knit another colour of yarn. With the simple push-button machines, you lay the second yarn by hand over selected needles and you can change that contrast yarn as you go across the row. This is not so easily done manually on the more complicated automatic machines (although it can be done, it is a bit of a fiddle). With thread lace (a facility that is not found on every automatic machine) some needles (again selected according to a charted or punch card pattern) knit one colour of yarn but the second yarn is always knitted by *all the needles*. In this type of patterning you will find some of the needles with both yarns in their stitches while others only have one yarn. If you use a very fine yarn for the second yarn, you will not be troubled with fine floats. The effect of thread

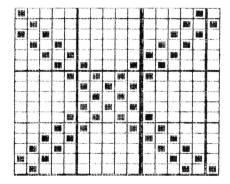

Fig. 20 Fair Isle stitch pattern

Fig. 21 Fair Isle stitch pattern used in photo 40

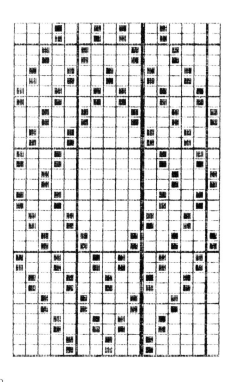

lace depends largely on the choice of yarns used.

We know that different types of wool felt to a different degree depending on all sorts of variables affecting the fibres. We have seen the difference in fabric when a sample is knitted in plain stocking stitch with rows of lamb's wool alternating with rows of Shetland wool. The Shetland felted and shrank less than the lamb's wool. I wanted to see what would happen in Fair Isle knitting if I kept the colour of the two yarns the same. I found that this largely depended on the choice of pattern. In the first sample the main yarn was the Shetland and the contrast was the lamb's wool (Fig. 20). The sample was knitted over 100 stitches and 100 rows at tension 6. It produced a fabric with a very nice surface which was bobbled and slightly textured on the stocking-stitch side. The fabric was very thick and stiff and could almost stand up on its own. It would make a lovely coat with very simple lines, but it had

no drape at all. The second sample was also knitted over 100 stitches and 100 rows at tension 6 (Fig. 21). The main yarn was lamb's wool and the contrast yarn was Shetland. The sample was not as thick but was still stiff and firm. It measured 22 cm wide and 21 cm long ($8\frac{1}{2} \times 8\frac{1}{4}$ in.) as opposed to the first sample which measured 19 cm wide and 18 cm long ($7\frac{1}{2} \times 7$ in.), so the final result was rather bigger but there was no visible pattern at all! What a disappointment (Photo 40). However, there are lessons to be learned and from the charted pattern you can tell how the proportion of one yarn to another can have a major effect on the final outcome.

To move on to other explorations, we can also felt fabric which has been knitted in the Fair Isle technique using mixed fibres. That is, one of the yarns can be wool which will felt and the other can be cotton, linen or a synthetic fibre which will not felt. This combination can produce some stunning and effective results.

40. Fair Isle using Shetland wool and lambswool felted

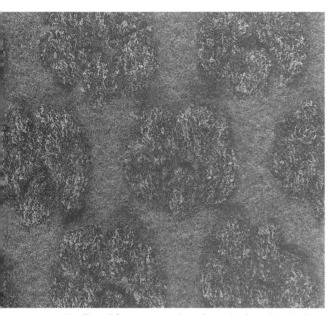

41. Fair Isle using wool and acrylic bouclé plied-up then felted

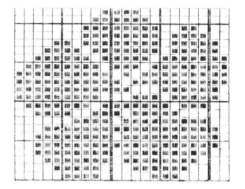

Fig. 22 Fair Isle stitch pattern used in photo 41

In the first sample of an all-over Fair Isle pattern, the main yarn was a fine wool in a single strand (Photo 41). The contrast yarn was a mixture of two strands of fine bouclé in two different colours. The sample was knitted over 100 stitches and 100 rows at tension 8 (Fig. 22). The large stitch size enabled the wool to felt nicely and it formed a very thick, soft and slightly fuzzy fabric. The type of felt formed depends largely on the quality of the wool fibres. The pattern which had been knitted in the double strands of fine bouclé did not felt and shrink and therefore bubbled up nicely and gave a three-dimensional effect to the surface. The major problem with making garments from this type of fabric is the floats. Because it is felt, the yarn is held firmly and, in theory, one could always cut the floats off after the felting process has been finished, but it would leave a very untidy backing. The best way of dealing with this problem is to line the garment with a separate fabric lining.

In the second sample using the same

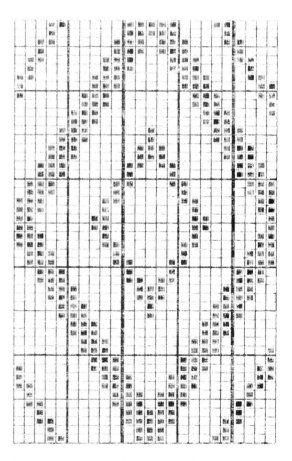

Fig. 23 Fair Isle stitch pattern used in photo 42

70

42. Another pattern using the same technique as in photo 41

combination of yarns the stitch pattern is altered (Fig. 23), giving a much more even all-over pattern with less bubbling. The effect is also quite striking and resembles the texture of a heavily brocaded fabric (Photo 42). This sample was knitted over 80 stitches and 100 rows but the resulting felt is wider than the previous sample knitted over 100 stitches. This is because of the stitch pattern. The fabric did not shrink as much in width as the first sample. On this sample, because of the stitch pattern, the floats hang out beyond the edge of the fabric and form very attractive loops along the edge. This might be used to great decorative effect when designing the garment. If you double the width and the length of the pattern you achieve a much more raised surface. The pattern becomes bolder and is a much stronger 'statement' (Fig. 24). This variation was knitted on the same number of needles (100) and rows (100) at a bigger tension (10). The result is a more striking patterned fabric (Photo 43). In this case the floats that appear at the edge are not attractive and must be removed when making the garment.

You must bear in mind that any stitch pattern you use will be considerably reduced during the felting process, so it is very important that all the designs you use for your knitted fabric are very large indeed (almost excessively large), to allow for the fact that they will shrink.

In addition to knitting an all-over Fair Isle

43. Another pattern using the same technique as in photo 41

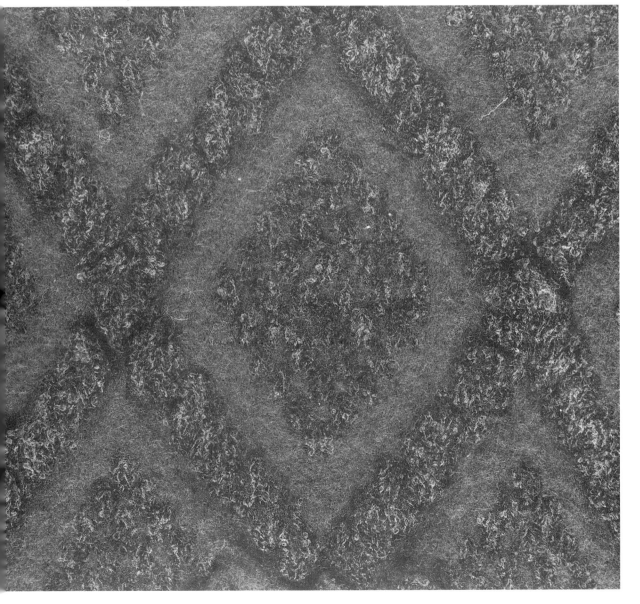

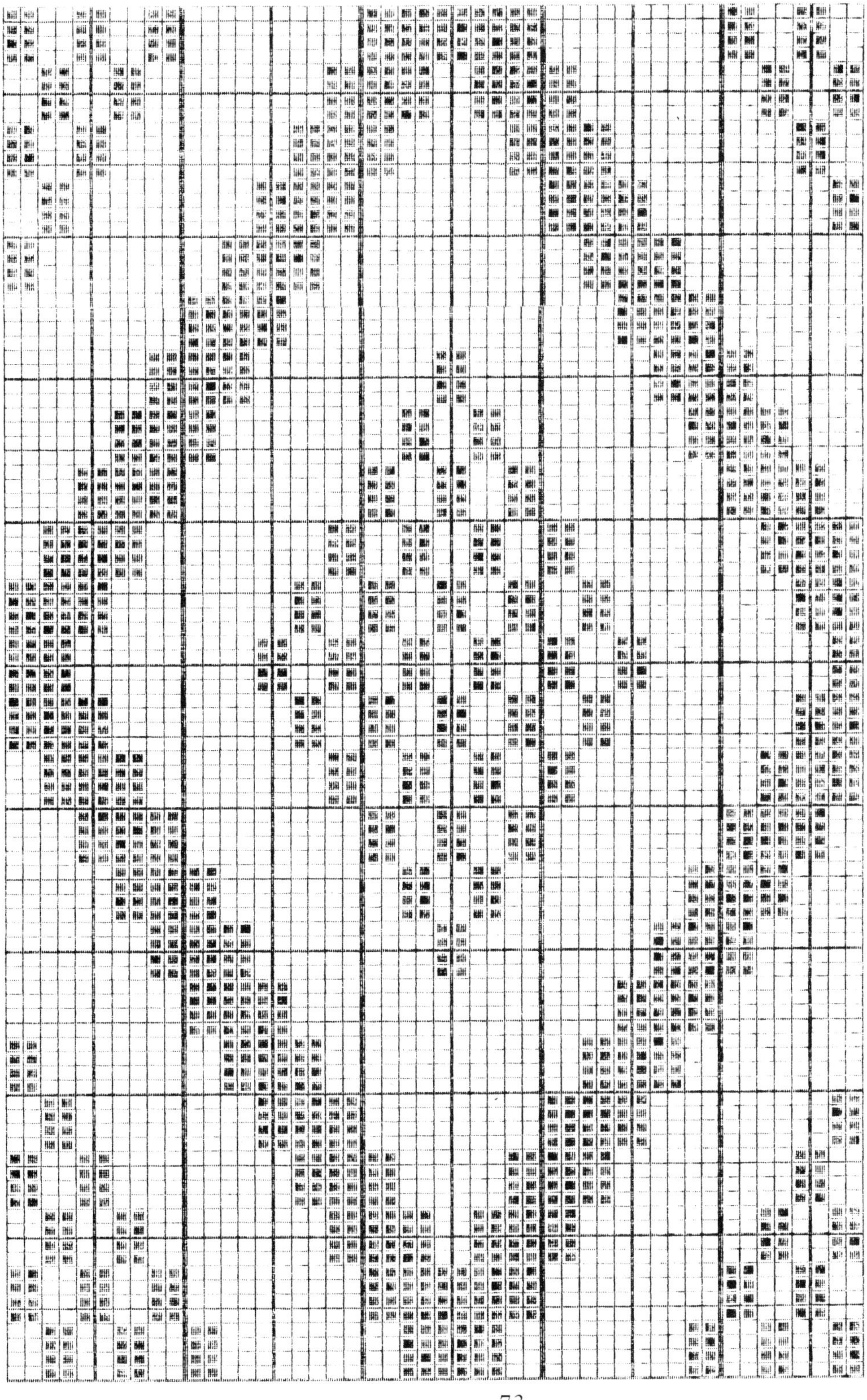

Fig. 24 Fair Isle
stitch pattern
used in photo 43

73

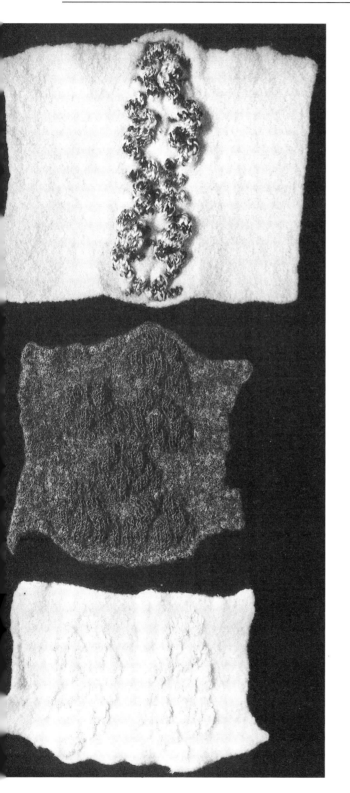

Fig. 25 Fair Isle stitch pattern used in photo 46

pattern, you can use a single motif to very good effect (Fig. 25). Single motifs carefully placed on the fabric to enhance the design of the garment can be very striking. In this sample a single strand of fine white botany yarn was used as the main yarn (Photo 46). The contrast yarn was a fairly fine, pure white, shiny rayon-type acrylic. The sample was knitted over 100 stitches and 80 rows at tension 10. When the stitch size is so big and the yarn is so fine, great care must be taken in putting this type of knitted fabric into the washing machine to felt because you run the risk of the knitting felting to itself and the final result being ruined. This swatch was pre-washed in Sansolaine, dried and then folded over. To facilitate even felting, the sample was sewn into a pocket all around the

44,45,46. Three samples showing a single motif Fair Isle, knitted using fine wool as the main yarn and an acrylic or rayon as the contrast

edges by hand, using ordinary sewing cotton. This particular sample did not felt to itself. This sort of motif knitting, used carefully and sparingly, would make a most attractive evening cape or wrap. It would suit a style that required a fabric with some body, as it does not drape well (Photo 46).

The next sample was knitted with the same botany yarn, but the first time the sample was made it felted to itself in the washing machine and the piece was a total disaster. At the second attempt, the fine botany used as the main yarn was used double (as two ends of yarn). The contrast colour in this case was a much thicker, multicoloured rayon yarn which results in a much more striking motif (Fig. 26). The characteristic of this type of motif is that it stands out in three dimensions without interfering with or distorting the felting of the surrounding knitted fabric (Photo 44). The motif is, in fact, distorted by the shrinking of the surrounding knitting during the process of felting. This fabric is really quite stiff and would be most suitable for a coat or jacket.

In the grey-and-blue sample the background yarn is an extremely fine grey botany wool, approximately 2/32 (Photo 45). The swatch was knitted over 80 stitches and 100 rows. The contrast yarn was a blue acrylic that had a 'mock cotton' look about it. Here again the motif technique was used in order to establish an isolated pattern. After it was finished the sample was rolled up in a fine cotton handkerchief and then sewn in, in the hopes that it would not come undone in the washing machine. It survived the first wash in the machine but didn't felt very satisfactorily, so it was put back again. The second time the felting was more even. After the second wash, the swatch was put in the tumble dryer for 10 minutes to finish it off. Really, with hindsight, I should have knitted

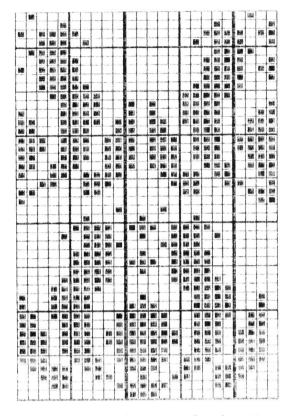

Fig. 26 Fair Isle stitch pattern used in photo 44

the swatch on a smaller tension or stitch size because the yarn is really very fine. The other alternative would be to use the main yarn doubled-up, but this would create a much thicker felted fabric.

Thread lace is designed to minimize the floats of a very fine second or contrast yarn when knitting a jacquard type of pattern. Because the second yarn is always knitted on all the needles, it never becomes a float. The main yarn is not knitted on some of the needles and it is this that creates a stitch pattern. In this sample you can see the contrast between the pattern knitted as a straightforward Fair Isle pattern and as a thread lace pattern (Photo 47). The colours of the two yarns are very different. In 'true' thread lace the colours of both yarns would

47. *Fair Isle using fine wool and acrylic yarn. The top pattern uses the thread lace technique*

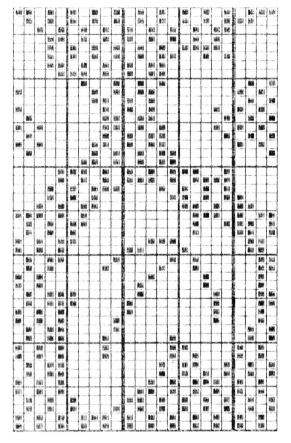

Fig. 27 'Leaves' Fair Isle stitch pattern used in photo 47

be the same, and the pattern would be achieved because of the difference in weight between the two yarns.

I used three stitch patterns (Figs. 27–29): in the first one, the pattern has disappeared completely. In the second pattern the 'flowers' are barely discernible but the texture of the fabric is really quite interesting even though the pattern is not very striking. You lose the shape of the flower itself but it forms quite an interesting three-dimensional 'bubble'.

The next section shows a pattern knitted as a straight Fair Isle and you can see the

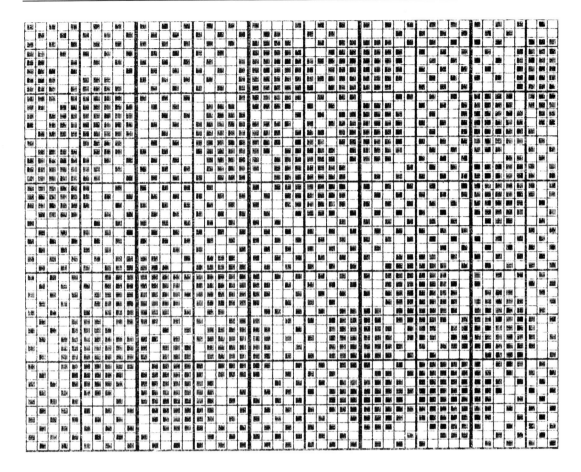

Fig. 28 'Flowers' Fair Isle stitch pattern used in photo 47

pattern quite clearly because of the contrast in the colour of the two yarns. The second yarn is a fine dark red bouclé and the main yarn is a fine white botany yarn. The wool felted to produce a firm, even fabric. The appearance of the individual stitches has totally disappeared and due to the texture of the bouclé, the pattern seems to emerge out of the matt, smooth, even-textured felted background, making quite an interesting fabric. In the following sample the same pattern was knitted with the same yarns and the same tension (6) but it was knitted as a thread lace pattern, and here you can quite

clearly see the difference between the effect of the two techniques. The thread lace is more muted and subtle and the fabric almost seems to be a tweed rather than a felt. Of course there are no floats to speak of on the back of this sample as there were in the previous sample.

In the next two samples, the colour of the wool and the colour of the fine acrylic bouclé was very close. The pattern consisted of large areas of a one-by-one needle selection and the thread lace pattern was almost totally lost (Fig. 30). The thread lace was knitted at tension 5, and the Fair Isle at

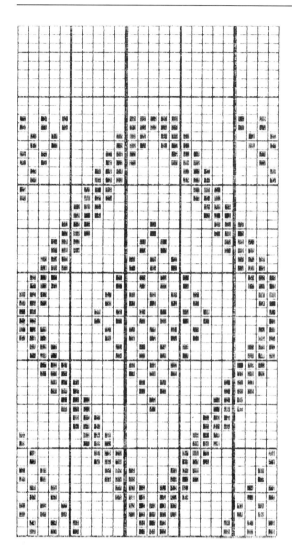

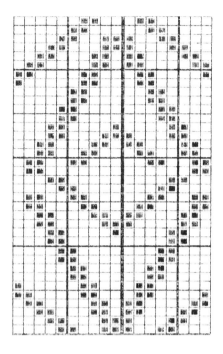

Fig. 29 (Left) 'Diamonds' Fair Isle stitch pattern used in photo 47
Fig. 30 (Above) Stitch pattern used as thread lace in photo 48

tension 8. The fabric was marginally more successful in the Fair Isle technique because there was no bouclé present in the felted areas, which resulted in a smoother contrast to the areas in the one-by-one pattern (Photo 48).

The last example in this group is a thread lace pattern which only has a small area of one-by-one patterning. The pattern lines are very simple and in this sample the thread lace is most effective. Three strands of fine wool have been used as the main yarn but,

Fig. 31 A garment with a felted yoke

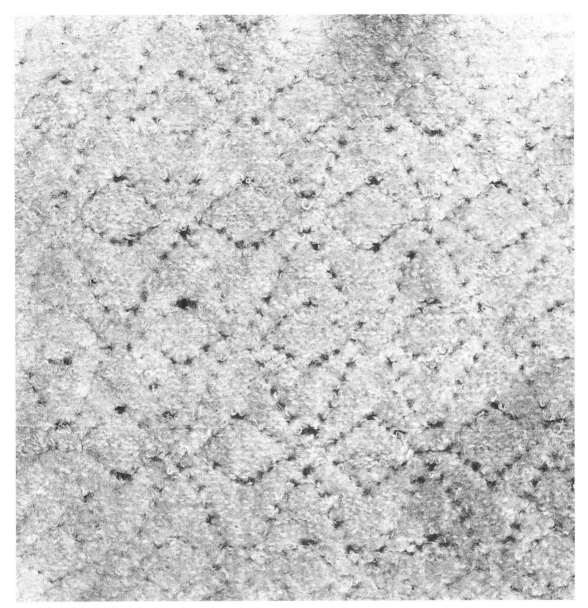

48. *Thread lace felted*

because they are all of different origin, the felted fabric is not smooth and homogeneous. The second yarn was an ordinary sewing cotton and while the felted result in no way resembles a lacy fabric, the technique has obviously produced an interesting sample. This pattern could be quite effectively doubled in width and length to produce a more striking and dynamic visual effect. As it is, the fabric is quite firm and rigid and would not drape well. It could be used for a decorative edge on a knitted garment such as the collar or a belt where stiffness would be required (Fig. 31).

Tuck and Weave Structures

Up to now we have considered the effect of felting on fabric which is primarily produced by knitting in stocking stitch. What happens when other stitch constructions are used to produce a knitted fabric which is then felted in the washing machine? Here again, if you are using a combination of fibres such as wool which will felt and a synthetic acrylic which will not felt, the proportion of one fibre to the other is critical in producing an interesting result.

The fabric produced by using tuck stitch does have a textural quality due to the fact that some stitches are 'gathered up' in the fabric. If you knit a tuck stitch pattern where the amount of wool yarn is much less than the amount of unfeltable yarn, the effect of washing the fabric in the washing machine is minimal. The only result is that you know your fabric is clean! Felting simply does not happen because there is not enough wool yarn to rub together, entangle itself and form a matted fabric. The stitches are still quite distinct. This can be very disappointing. The structure of the stitch creates a textural fabric and leads you to believe that this three-dimensional effect will be emphasized in the felting process. You may think

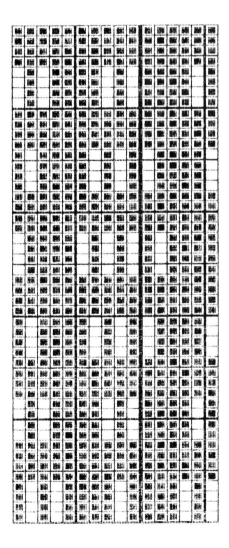

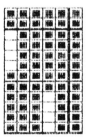

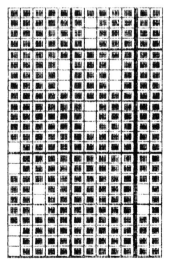

Figs. 32–34 Stitch patterns used as tuck stitch. The blank squares represent tuck stitches

that the wool must shrink and make the acrylic bobbles stand out even more. In the samples illustrated you can see that this simply is not the case. I have tried different stitch patterns with a variety of different yarns and the total effect of felting is practically nil (Figs. 32–34). It is a pleasant fabric and easy to handle, but it is not felt!

In the last sample the effect is rather more exciting and pronounced (Photo 49). By doubling the length of the stitch pattern, I managed to achieve some textural excitement, and by exchanging the yarn that is tucking for the yarn that is knitting, there is some variety in the surface of the pattern (Figs. 35–37). It seems obvious that a simple

49. Tuck stitch using fine wool and acrylic, felted

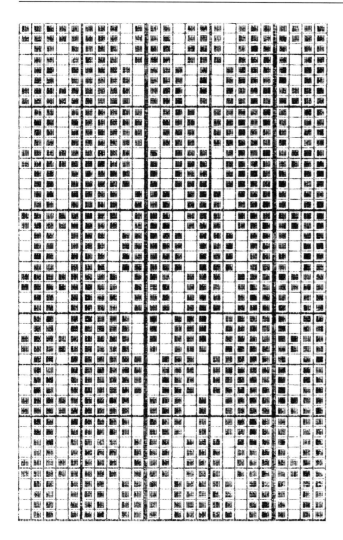

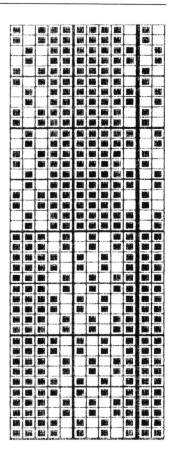

Fig. 35–36 Stitch patterns used as tuck stitch. The blank squares represent tuck stitches

pattern in a plain repeat with only isolated needles tucking results in the most effective fabric for felting. If you consistently have the same needles tucking and others consistently knitting you will produce a fabric with some interesting possibilities. It is, of course, up to you to follow your own experimental road and see where it leads you.

Felting woven fabric has produced some surprises too. I chose to experiment briefly with weaving in strips of torn nylon fabric (Photo 50). The sample illustrated was knit-

ted over 100 stitches and 105 rows at tension 6 on a standard-gauge machine. Needles were selected by hand in a one-by-one checkerboard pattern row by row. The fabric strips were laid in by hand using an intarsia weaving method. That is, the weaving area was controlled not by the automatic patterning on the machine but by selecting the areas for laying in the yarn by hand. The patterns or areas could be developed in design work on paper first and then the pattern placed in the knit-leader/tracer/ radar to assist you in executing the intarsia

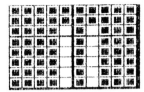

Fig. 37 Stitch pattern used as tuck stitch. The blank squares represent tuck stitches

weaving. In the areas where there was a lot of weaving the woollen yarn did not felt at all, and only felted in the areas where there was no weaving, which resulted in quite an interesting effect in the fabric. It pushes out to make a bowl shape. This distortion of the fabric caused by the proportion of nylon strips woven in with the wool opens the door on a whole new range of possibilities for experimentation. Of course, the more predictable results are produced where the fabric is wrapped loosely around one or two needles and then the woollen yarn merely holds the weaving strips in place. It felts quite nicely in this area because there are not enough of the weaving strips to impede the felting process. The weaving strips almost embellish the surface of the felt as if it had been embroidered.

Some ideas for future experimentation might be to weave in wool yarn with an acrylic background; to follow up and extend the idea of intarsia weaving to produce a distorted fabric which might lead to interesting garment shapes; and to weave one type of wool onto a background knit in another type of wool. Weaving can be done vertically as well as horizontally, so you can have totally different yarns weaving up your work as you knit.

Another possibility for experimentation would be to explore the use of slip stitch when you construct a fabric which contains a three-dimensional quality. By choosing your yarns carefully you will be able to exaggerate the three-dimensional effect. But be warned: the effect you achieve may not always be the effect you have predicted! Be very sure you keep an open mind about your experimenting and do not look at your sample as if to say, 'What am I telling this piece of knitting?'. Rather, look at it as if to say, 'What is this piece of knitting trying to tell *me*?'

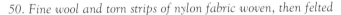

50. *Fine wool and torn strips of nylon fabric woven, then felted*

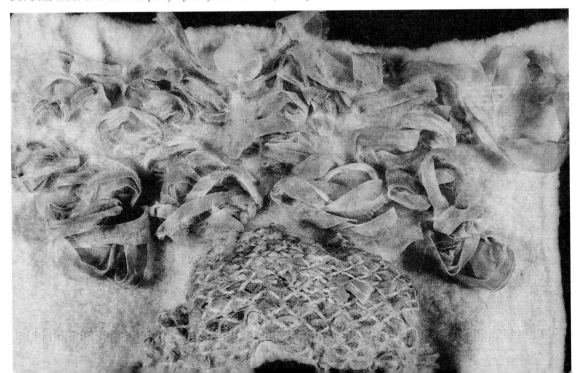

Double-bed Techniques

Up to now we have been mainly concerned with techniques that can be achieved on a single-bed knitting machine. Now we will begin to explore the possibilities of fabric produced using a double-bed machine. As in the earlier sections, here we are only touching the tip of the iceberg.

With the double-bed fabric you do not have the same kinds of technical problem that you do with single-bed fabric. That is, the fabric is not inclined to roll up when it is removed from the machine, and you do not need to take special precautions to ensure that it does not felt with thick, rolled edges – but then you may have other problems. The fabric will be much thicker when you are knitting it on both beds. You will not be able to lay-in small areas of pattern by hand with both beds in use, and you may find it difficult to knit a very fine yarn on a double bed in a large stitch size.

It can prove rather difficult to use a fine yarn on a double-bed machine which relies on weighting to pull the stitches down off the needles (as opposed to the single-bed machine which relies on the brushes below the sinker plate to push the stitches down off the needles). If your stitch size is too big you will find the stitches jumping off the needles and running back down your fabric. The

solution to this problem in the first place is to be very careful when you work your tension swatch. You want to know from the sample, not from the garment, if you are going to have a problem. Then, if your stitches are jumping off the needles you can either adjust the stitch size by making it smaller (try first one bed and then the other), or you can try hanging more weights on your fabric. But do be careful. More weights may mean more shredded yarn and accidentally torn knitting. You can also cause more trouble if you hang too many weights onto your knitted fabric.

When you are casting on with a very fine, delicate yarn, the cast-on comb and the weights can often tear the yarn to shreds and you find that instead of having the first zigzag row you merely have a row of 'spaghetti'. If you have difficulty in casting on with a fine yarn, you can always cast on with an acrylic yarn which is stronger and more even-tempered. After the fabric has been felted, you will in any case be cutting away this unwanted selvage which has been knitted with waste yarn.

The other factor you must bear in mind when knitting any Fair Isle pattern on the machine is the degree to which the pattern shrinks after it has been felted (Fig. 38). In

Fig. 38 Fair Isle Stitch Pattern used in photo 51

51. *Double-bed fabric before and after felting*

the 'before' and 'after' samples the two swatches were knitted exactly the same at tension 6/6 (6 on the main bed and 6 on the ribber) (Photo 51). They were both done with a striping backing. That is, every needle on the ribber knits every row, so for every two complete rows knitted on the main bed, 4 rows were knitted on the ribber. The unfelted sample measures 48 cm wide by 33.5 cm (19 × 13 in.) long. The felted sample measured 26.5 cm wide by 15 cm long (10½ × 6 in.). Not every sample you knit will felt in exactly the same way. This is why it is so important for you to carry out your own experiments with your own wool and your own stitch construction. With a much larger pattern you would have problems dealing with floats on single-bed knitting but when you are using the ribber in conjunction with your main bed you can eliminate the float problem.

With Pfaff/Passap machines, double-bed fabric is very easy to do and the fact that weighting the knitting is not vital can make

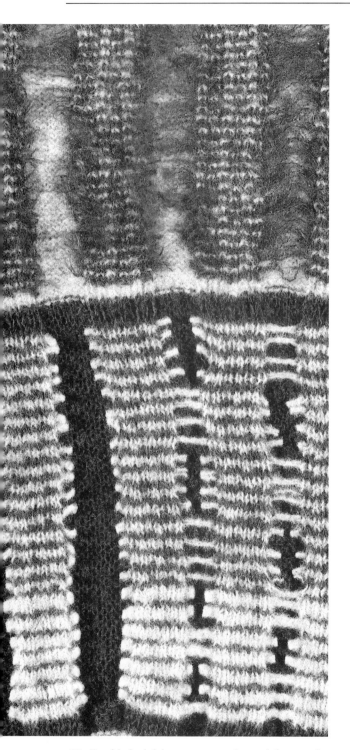

the job of producing a fabric with a fine yarn and a large stitch size much easier. However, if you are having problems with dropped stitches due to the use of a rather large stitch size, there is nothing to stop you from hanging a few weights on here and there just to help your knitting along a bit. You may find this will just do the trick when knitting a difficult bit of fabric.

When you are using a combination of yarns on your double-bed fabric you can produce some interesting and unusual results by subsequently felting your knitting (Photo 52). The first sample relies upon needle arrangement to create a fabric pattern (Fig. 39). You may need a colour changer to execute this variation because you will be changing your yarn every two rows. Arrange all the needles on one bed to working position and arrange the needles on the opposite bed so that 6 are working and 6 are not working. If you knit a plain fabric with this needle set-up you would get vertical lines of ribbing.

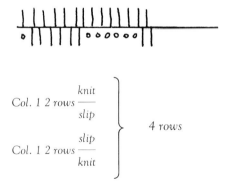

52. Double-bed fabric using acrylic and fine wool, felted

Fig. 39 Needle arrangement for double-bed fabric

Set the carriages so that the bed with all needles in working position knits 2 rows with one yarn and slips the next 2 rows with the second yarn while the bed with only some of the needles in working position knits all the yarn all the time. You may have to change the cam box or carriage setting every two rows to achieve this effect. In one sample, the acrylic is the main or background yarn and the wool is the contrast stripes. In the second sample it is the other way round. The floats between the ribbed sections are cut after the sample has been felted in the washing machine. In the sample where the wool has formed floats, when they have felted they are short and stumpy and pull the acrylic backing into puffs where they have not been cut through. In the sample where the wool forms the felt background, it has shrunk and the acrylic floats have been cut and brushed to create quite a nice effect. They are also quite attractive where they have been brushed and not cut. This sample illustrates how important it is to use the right kind of yarn in the right situation and how easy it is for the choice of yarn to make or break a good idea.

You will really need to have a very good idea of exactly how your machine works to be able to explore the felting possibilities in double-bed work to the limit. If you can produce a jacquard pattern on one bed, with a plain fabric knitted on the second bed, you have gone a long way towards creating interesting textures using a combination of a variety of yarns. The next sample is knitted in a full needle rib set up over 80 stitches on the main bed and 100 rows at tension 6/6 (Fig. 40). It is knitted as a double-bed jacquard, but the second bed will knit only the woollen yarn, so it is set to slip for two rows every other two rows when the acrylic yarn is in the feeder and is being knitted on the main or patterning bed. When the sample is put into the washing machine to be felted, the stitches knitted in acrylic yarn will bubble up, but the backing fabric which is now felted will be smooth and firm. This does result in a very interesting double-sided fabric which could be used as a trim or as the

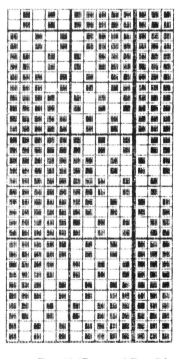

53. *Double-bed jacquard, using acrylic as the contrast and fine wool as the main yarn, felted*

Fig. 40 'Zig-zags' Fair Isle stitch pattern used in photo 53

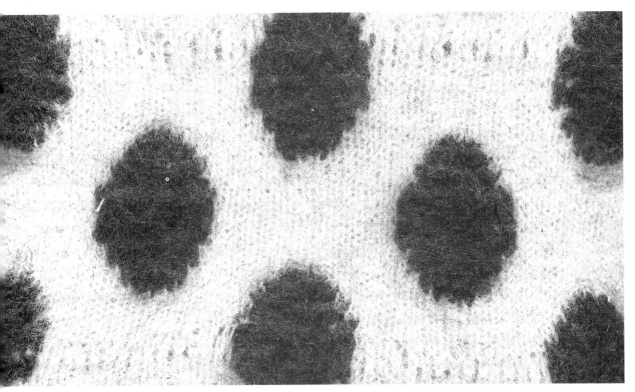

54. Double-bed jacquard, using acrylic as the contrast and fine wool as the main yarn, with the backing knitted in acrylic only, felted

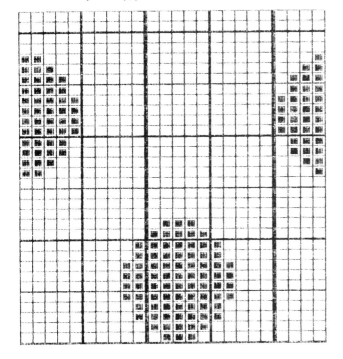

Fig. 41 'Bubbles' Fair Isle stitch pattern used in photo 54

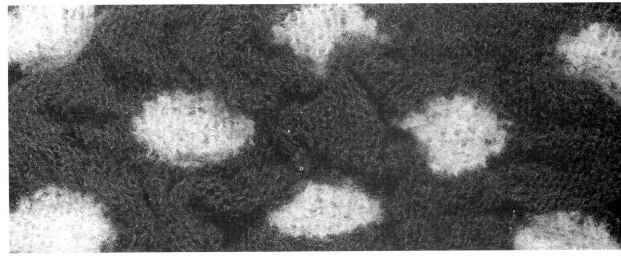

55. *As in photo 54, with the yarns reversed and the backing knitted in wool only*

primary fabric for a garment (Photo 53). Because the proportion of acrylic fibre to wool fibre is quite generous, the fabric is not too thick and stiff. It is quite firm and reluctant to drape, but it is not very heavy. Of course the handle depends a great deal on the type of acrylic you use.

The next two samples use the same technique and yarns (Photos 54–55). The stitch pattern has been chosen to take advantage of the differential felting factor of each type of yarn (Fig. 41). The variations are the dots and backing on the second bed which are knitted in one yarn (either the acrylic or the wool) while the background of the pattern is knitted in the alternative yarn. Here you can see quite clearly that the wool has made the acrylic fabric bubble up quite considerably. Two other possibilities which might be tried would be to use the same yarn for the background of the pattern and for the backing knitted on the second bed, giving two more alternatives that could be tried with this technique. You may find the fabric so interesting when you have begun to experiment that you have a great deal of difficulty in making a final choice as to which fabric to use in your garment (Fig. 42).

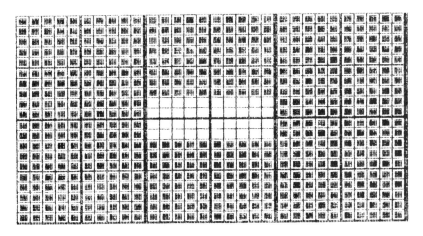

Fig. 42 'Dashes' Fair Isle stitch pattern

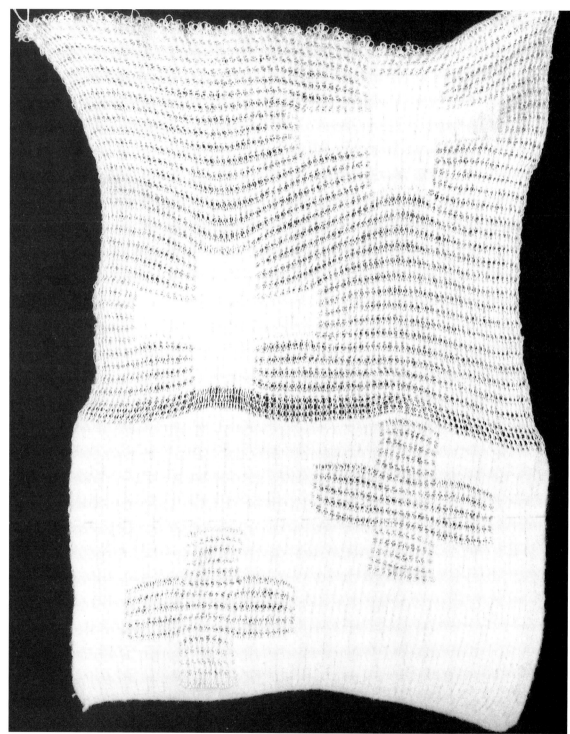

56. Double-bed jacquard using a striped backing, felted. The top sample uses wool as the contrast and acrylic as the main yarn. In the bottom sample the yarns are reversed

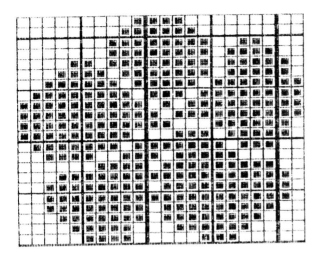

Fig. 43 'Flowers' Fair Isle stitch pattern

These variations are possible when you can control and set your ribber to produce variations on the standard double-bed jacquard technique. But the sort of fabric you can produce using the standard techniques for the double bed and just combining yarns of different compositions can also be quite interesting and challenging. Here are several samples using a fine wool and a fine acrylic with a striped background knitted on the ribber. Large, simple patterns show up most effectively (Figs. 43–44). You can also use a fine wool and a very fine multicoloured cotton yarn. In this case, the wool will shrink and the little cotton stitches will bubble up to give a very interesting texture to your fabric. You can reverse the main and contrast yarns, especially with larger motifs, to achieve a totally different type of fabric just using the ordinary double-bed jacquard technique. In these two samples knitted with fine wool and fine acrylic yarn you can see how a simple large motif can be very striking and effective. In one section the wool was the

Fig. 44 'Sprawling Flowers' Fair Isle stitch pattern

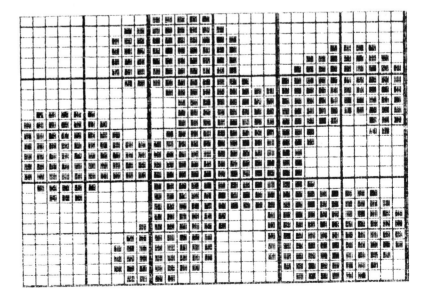

57. *Release stitch using wool and acrylic, felted*

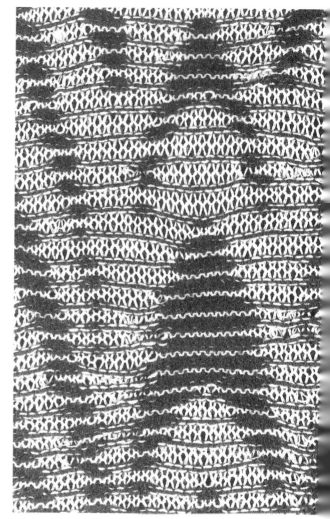

58. *Sample in photo 57, from the purl side*

main yarn and the acrylic the contrast, and in the other section vice versa (Photo 56, Fig. 46).

A variation on this technique produces what I consider to be a most striking and unusual fabric. Cast on in the usual way but be sure to hang your comb so that the teeth are placed to hang on the loops between each of the needles on the ribber. (If you do not get your comb to hang on these loops do not worry unduly because it will not make a great deal of difference.) Knit your double-bed jacquard in the usual way, making sure

you use the simple striping backing technique on the second bed. (That is, all the needles on this bed knit all the stitches all the time on every row.) When you have finished your knitting, *drop all the stitches on the main or patterning bed and allow them to run back to the beginning of the knitting.* You may cast off the stitches that are remaining on your second bed. When you come to felt this fabric you must enclose it completely in muslin. Fold the muslin over the fabric and roll it up. Then place it in the washing machine at 30°C (86°F) on a normal wash and

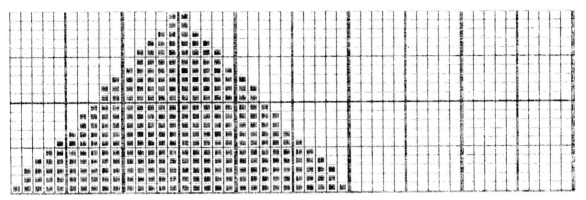

Fig. 45 'Pyramid' Fair Isle stitch pattern used in photo 59

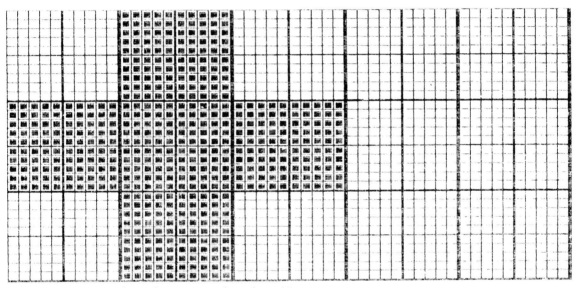

Fig. 46 'Cross' Fair Isle stitch pattern used in photo 56

allow it to felt in the usual way. If after the first try it is not felted completely it can be returned for another wash without the performance with the muslin. This does produce a most unusual and exciting fabric (Photos 57–59, Figs. 45, 47). It is felt which is light and airy – it is felt which is not felt!

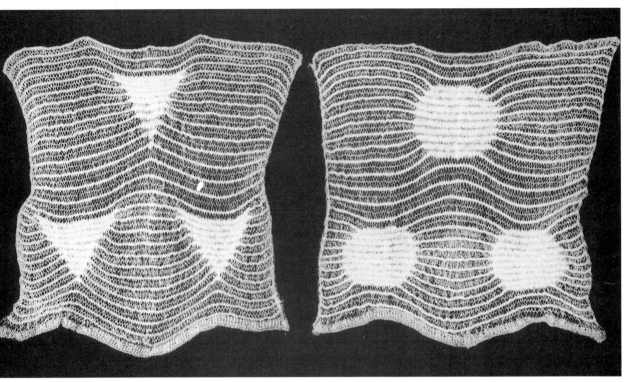

59. *Two samples of release stitch using fine wool and acrylic, felted*

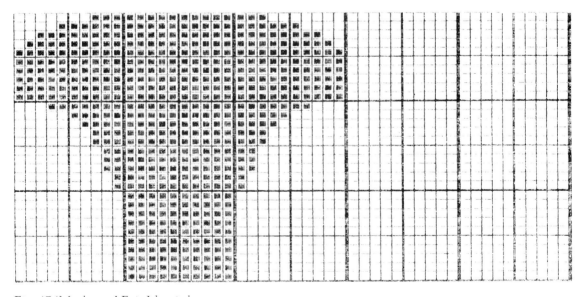

Fig. 47 'Mushroom' Fair Isle stitch pattern

The Projects

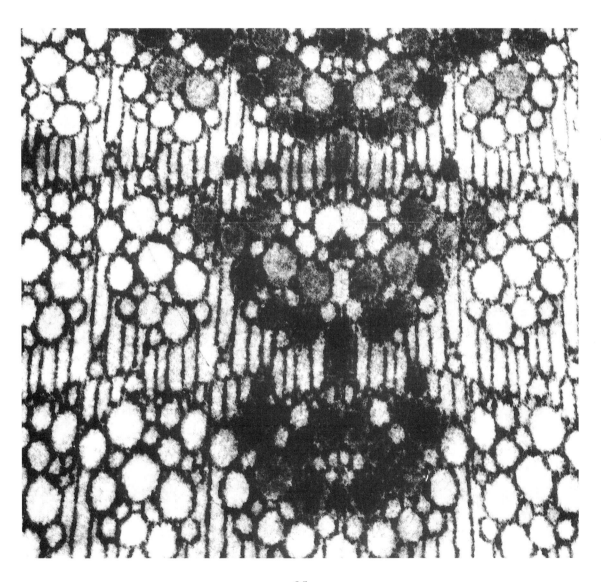

Introduction

How did I discover the process of felting? Why should a machine knitter do what most would think sacrilegious: put a good bit of knitted wool into a washing machine? Plenty of us have thrown a good wool jumper into the machine by mistake and been horrified when a garment only big enough to fit a doll and stiff as a board emerged. I had seen articles and pamphlets on 'boiled wool' and not been moved to follow their instructions – a 'boiled wool' jacket had never really appealed to me. I had read how to knit up a whole cone of good fine wool the width of the needle bed, place the resulting length of knitted fabric into the washing machine on a hot wash, remove the result, cut it up and sew it into a dressing gown. I was not interested in knitting dressing gowns, never mind going to all the trouble of knitting a plain fabric that would then have to be shrunk and cut and sewn into a dressing gown which would probably be too stiff to be comfortable anyway. I did not fancy knitting a jumper too big and then felting that, because I could not be sure exactly how much and where the garment would shrink. I like to be in control of my knitting, and that process seemed much too risky to me.

So, back to the original question – why felt? I was on a shopping jaunt in an expensive boutique when I saw it. 'It' was a jacket by Missoni. It was wonderful: it was navy blue and white and had a pattern which resembled the Japanese print of a wave on it. It was very expensive. It was felted knitting! I was hooked. I rushed home and began to experiment. I knitted dozens of swatches 100 stitches by 100 rows, trying out all sorts of yarns and all sorts of stitch constructions. When I had finished a few swatches I would throw them into the washing machine with our normal wash. Our washing machine is always set at 30°C (86°F). I took no extra care with the swatches. We had very clean clothes that summer! In fact we could not get the clothes dirty enough quick enough to keep up with the swatch production! Eventually I found putting a plimsoll or flip-flop into the machine with the swatches was a good substitute for the additional clothes. Once I was on my way, there was no holding me back. There is still a great deal of exploring left to do but here are some ideas that you might like to put into practice on the way.

Blue and white jacket

Fabric paint on felt

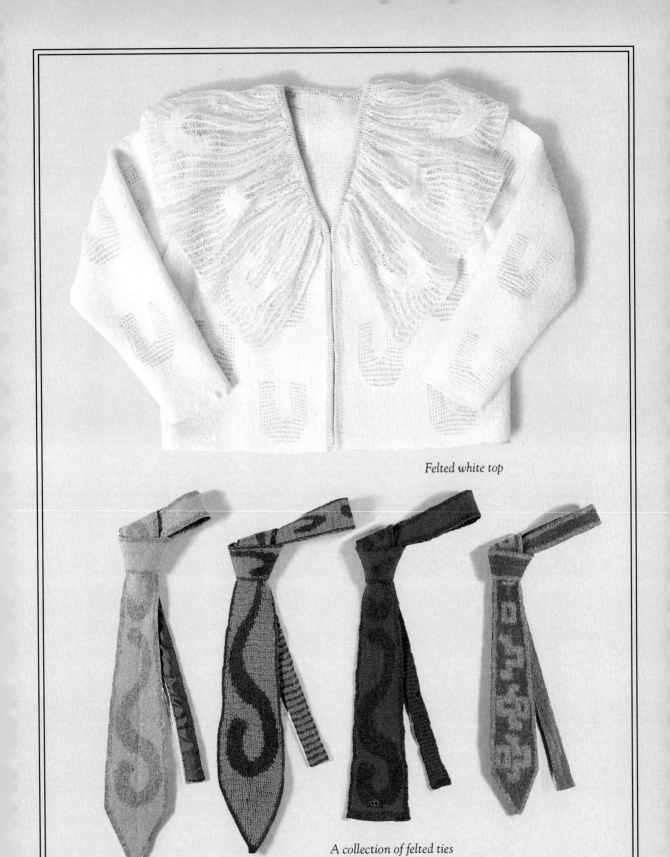

Felted white top

A collection of felted ties

Maroon raglan jacket

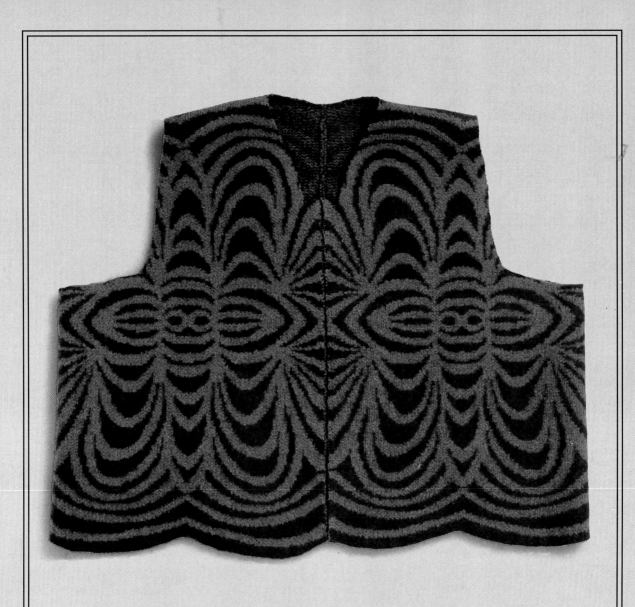

Green waistcoat

Grey waistcoat

Blue and red cape

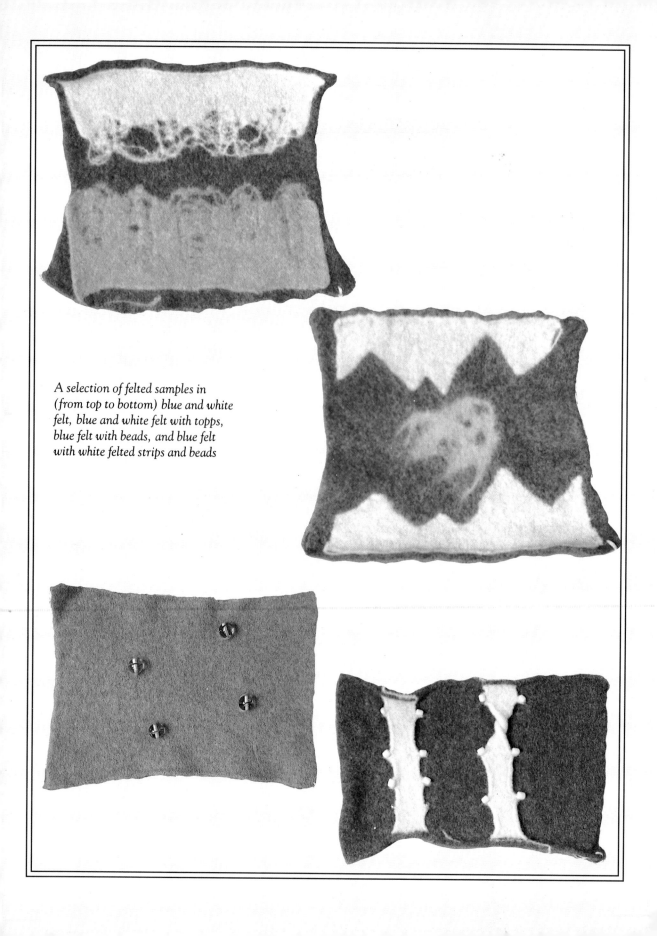

A selection of felted samples in (from top to bottom) blue and white felt, blue and white felt with topps, blue felt with beads, and blue felt with white felted strips and beads

Ties

One of the best ways of beginning your journey into felting is to start with a small item. You could felt up a sample and make it into a little bag or a change purse. These would be quite useful as small presents, but it might be a good idea to tackle something a bit bigger – an item that required a bit of shaping, perhaps. Here are four examples of knitted felted ties. Two of the ties have been shaped on the machine. The other two were knitted as single motifs and cut out after being felted (see colour pages).

The first step in making a tie is to establish a tie pattern (Fig. 48). You can buy a sewing pattern, or you could make a tracing from a bought tie. They vary in width but are usually consistent in length (Fig. 51).

The ties pictured here were all knitted in the double-bed jacquard technique (Photo 60). The fabric produced by this technique is more stable than a single-bed fabric and will lend itself to designs suitable for ties. The designs are done on paper and then transferred to a punch card or mylar sheet.

A swatch must be knitted over 100 stitches and 100 rows and then felted. It is a good idea to weigh the yarn before knitting

60. Four ties

97

the swatch. If you weigh it again after the tie is completed you will know how much yarn you need to knit one tie. Measure your swatch after it has been felted. This measurement will tell you how many stitches and rows you need to knit to make your tie.

For example, if 100 stitches = 25 cm you must divide 100 by 25 to find out how many stitches there are in 1 cm. In this case you would have 4 stitches in 1 cm. If your tie was 8 cm at its widest point you would need 32 stitches for the width of your tie. If you wanted to knit a narrower tie – 6 cm, for example – you could get the width of your pattern onto a 24-stitch repeat punch card.

In any case you could make the stitch pattern a single motif and select the edge needles by hand to knit the outline of the tie in the contrast colour. You would need to 'write a pattern' for your tie if you wanted to have the outline knitted in a contrast colour, but if you were happy without this type of edging you could just knit the required length in your pattern and cut the tie out afterwards. On machines that have a pre-select row – that is, where the needles that knit the contrast colour are selected to UWP by the pass of the carriage (or where the pushers for the needles are selected by the pass of the cam box) – you can pro-

98

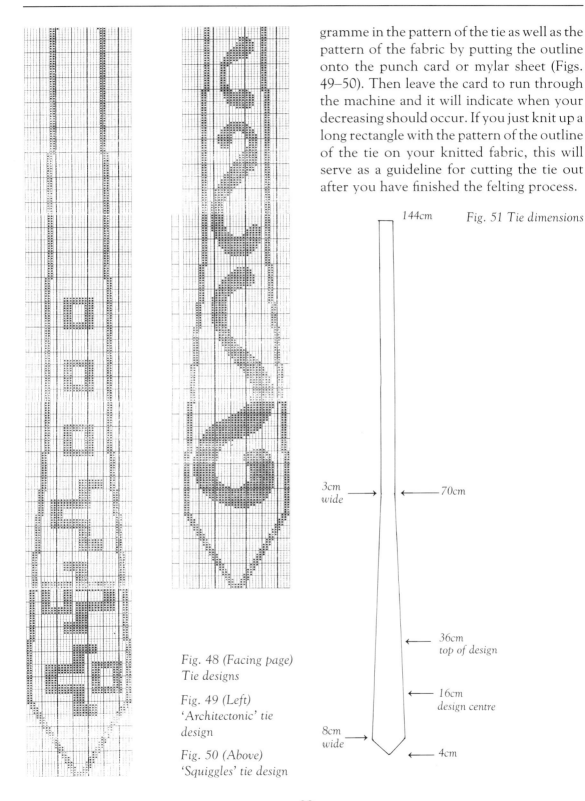

gramme in the pattern of the tie as well as the pattern of the fabric by putting the outline onto the punch card or mylar sheet (Figs. 49–50). Then leave the card to run through the machine and it will indicate when your decreasing should occur. If you just knit up a long rectangle with the pattern of the outline of the tie on your knitted fabric, this will serve as a guideline for cutting the tie out after you have finished the felting process.

144cm

Fig. 51 Tie dimensions

3cm wide

70cm

36cm top of design

16cm design centre

8cm wide

4cm

Fig. 48 (Facing page) Tie designs

Fig. 49 (Left) 'Architectonic' tie design

Fig. 50 (Above) 'Squiggles' tie design

99

It would help in making the design for the tie if you drew out your design and sizing information onto graph paper before you transferred it to the punch card or mylar sheet. This would give you an idea of how it would look. Remember that you need not have the pattern up the whole length of the tie. It can be plain beyond the point where the knot would be tied. If you make a slight mistake in the length of your tie you can always cut a bit off the straight end or you can pin out the tie and press it with a steam iron to lengthen it a bit.

When you are ready to felt your knitted tie it is wise to take certain precautions before putting it into the washing machine. It is a very long, thin piece of knitting. (However, if you plan to go into production you could always knit a wide piece of machine knitting with several ties 'knitted-in' as patterns like a 'cloth kit', and then cut them out afterwards.) To discourage the edges from rolling in on themselves you could steam press them. Then you might sew them up in a length of muslin or just sew them edge to edge loosely with sewing cotton. They will then felt more easily and you will not get a 'fluted' edge which may have to be cut off and would ruin the tie.

To finish the tie you have a number of choices. If you have made it in double-bed jacquard it will be quite a firm fabric but it might become distorted if tied frequently so it is probably a good idea to back it. You can use an iron-on facing or Vilene on the back. You can cut a lining a little bit wider than the tie, turn in the edges and hand sew it down around the edge of your tie, or you can cut a lining which is the same size as your tie, place right sides together and seam it down into a tube leaving an opening at the narrow end to pull the tube through so that the right side of the fabric is on the outside.

Blue and Red Cape

This cape is quite a dramatic garment. This is probably because the pattern for it is so big. The garment shape that inspired it was from a commercial Vogue sewing pattern. The reason it appealed to me was that the shape was simple, dramatic and elegant and needed very little modification. It was, however, very wide. But if I could sew my knitted fabric together before putting it into the washing machine to felt it, I could make the fabric as wide as I wanted. I weighed the yarn first and then knitted a test swatch in a similar type of double-bed jacquard pattern over 100 stitches and 100 rows at tension 6/6, and measured it. I calculated I would need to knit 200 stitches and 450 (900) rows in double-bed jacquard fabric to knit one half of the front. Before felting, the knitted piece measured nearly 2.5 m (8 ft) in length. The two fronts were sewn together loosely by hand with sewing cotton around the edges to encourage them to felt evenly. The two pieces for the back were joined up the centre back seam using the same yarn used to knit the garment. The remaining edges were sewn up as the front. The garment was felted in the washing machine in the usual way. The stitch pattern for one of the four sections was 200 stitches wide and 450 (900) rows long. I then decided to design a stitch pattern which would cover the whole area to be knitted as if it were a single motif. I drew out the outline of the garment shape that would be cut out of the felted fabric and then I designed that motif to fit into this shape and echo the outline. Areas that would eventually be cut away had no patterning on them. The design finally covered 12 mylar sheets for an electronic knitting machine (Fig. 52). The edging was a knitted braid which was sewn on by hand. Although the colours were fast, when the fabric was felted the colours seemed to blend into each other, giving a nice muted effect to the pattern (see colour pages). The two shoulder seams and the underarm seams were finished on the right side of the garment and subsequently covered over with tuck-stitch single-bed knitted braid. This garment is also wonderfully warm and easy to wear. Do remember to weigh the yarn that you have left over after you have finished your knitting in order to calculate how much yarn you have used. Subtract the yarn you have left from the yarn you had when you started out.

If your felted pieces show some discrepancy in size after they have been processed in the washing machine, you can block them out carefully to size by pinning them out on a board while they are still wet and allowing them to dry to the correct shape. You can also mould them to a three-dimensional shape while they are still wet and they will retain that shape after they have dried.

By weighing the yarn both before and after the garment was made I found that I had used 175 g (6 oz) of red yarn and 600 g (21 oz) of blue yarn. The dimensions of one panel before felting was 107 cm by 64 cm (42 × 25 in.); after felting it was 74 cm by 41 cm (29 × 16 in.).

Fig. 52 (Overleaf) Stitch pattern for the cape

Blue and White Jacket

This jacket was inspired by Dutch stencilled flower motifs. It was knitted as a double-bed jacquard fabric. The garment pattern used was a commercial sewing pattern. I chose one with a very simple shape. The fabrics recommended for the pattern were fleece, blanket wool, tweed, flannel, double knits, melton and double-faced fabrics. There were no facings included in the pattern and the edges were to be covered with a continuous bias binding.

First I weighed the yarn I was planning to use. If I weighed it before and after I would have a good idea of exactly how much yarn I had used in the garment as it was to be a two-colour jacquard stitch pattern.

Then I knitted a test square using a stitch pattern that would be similar to the pattern I planned to use in the garment. After felting I measured the swatch and calculated how many stitches and rows I would need for each garment piece. The felt had to be bigger than the paper pattern piece because the edges were not usable and would have to be cut off, so I had to allow quite a bit for 'wastage'.

Next I had to determine exactly where I wanted the stitch pattern on the garment. I knew how many rows I would have to knit, and the number of rows in the stitch pattern would leave me with a blank area where I could place a border at the bottom (Fig. 53). This border could also be used in the smaller sections which would not take the bigger pattern, so I used the leaves on the side inserts and at the cuff of the sleeves.

The pieces were then knitted, felted, and cut out. But how to construct this garment? There are several sewing techniques that can be used to make up a felted jacket. I decided to use a felled seam which came onto the right side of the garment and then to cover this seam with a decorative braid that had been knitted on the machine using the same yarn I had used for the jacket. As the jacket was knitted using the double bed I decided to make the braid and trimming in full needle rib. The braid covering the seams was knitted and then sewn on using the sewing machine. The edging was knitted using a full needle rib with one needle on one of the beds in the centre of the braid in non-working position to give a foldline. This was also sewn on using the sewing machine. There is a closing at the neck which is just a loop of braid sewn onto the edge of the jacket that loops over a button sewn onto the collar. There are two sets of small hooks and eyes which are located further down on the front edge of the jacket but because they are very small they are not noticeable. I wanted the pattern to match across the front of the jacket without being marred by buttons or buttonholes. The felted fabric for this jacket is very stiff and rigid. It keeps its shape and wears very well. It is also extremely warm and comfortable (see colour pages).

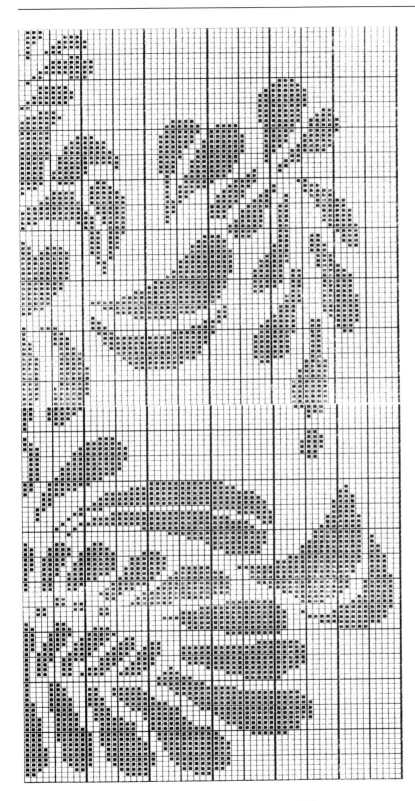

Fig. 53 Stitch pattern for the blue and white jacket

Grey Waistcoat

This garment was designed to be knitted on a single-bed machine using a 24-stitch repeat punch card. The floats on the fabric are very small and the result is a fine, smooth, soft, thick felt fabric.

The garment shape chosen for this waistcoat is very simple indeed. It must be remembered that any felted garment is likely to be worn over other clothes, so a good deal of allowance must be made when calculating how wide the garment will be. In this case the garment is 120 cm (47 in.) wide designed to fit a 91 cm (36 in.) bust. In other words, the garment should be about 30% larger than the bust size to make a felted garment that will be roomy, comfortable and becoming. Because of the width required for this garment, the back was knitted in two sections. This allowed a variation in the stitch pattern so that the diagonal lines met at a V in the middle of the back. The two knitted pieces were joined on the linker using the same wool as was used to knit the garment. The remaining sides of the two back pieces were sewn up loosely by hand using sewing cotton. Then the piece was felted. It was put, on its own, into the washing machine on a normal cycle, halfload (low water level), with Sansolaine at 30°C (86°F). When it was removed the sewing thread could easily be cut through and the piece opened out. The centre back seam had felted totally and there was no indication of a seam on the right side. The bottom edges had fluted slightly and were cut off. The front had to be made much longer because the collar for the left side was cut off the right and the collar for the right side was cut off the left (Fig. 54). It was then joined with a seam up the centre back (not an invisible seam) on the sewing machine and the collar was placed on the neck edge of the waistcoat wrong side to right side (Fig. 55). This meant that when the collar was folded back the right side would be showing. All the seams were sewn to be felled on the right side of the garment and were then covered with a tuck-stitch braid which was knitted on the single-bed machine using the same grey yarn that was used to knit the garment. The edges were also covered with the same type of braid, but this had to be knitted wider in order to fold over the edge. When seams are finished on the right side, the inside of your garment has a very neat, professional appearance, even if you do not wish it to be reversible (see colour pages).

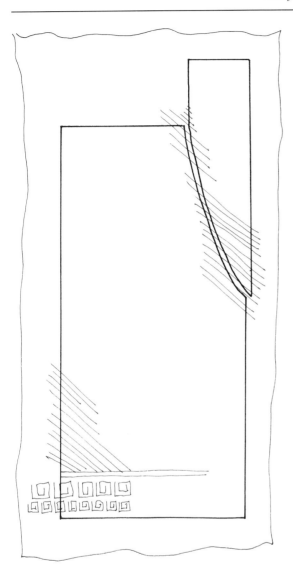

Fig. 54 Cutting off the collar from one side of the front

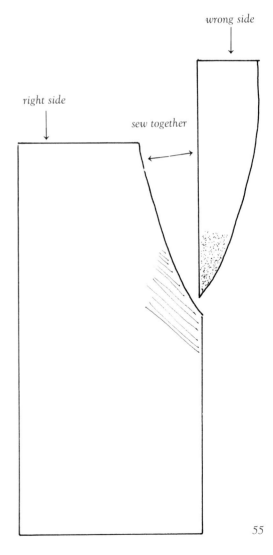

Fig. 55 Sewing the collar on to the opposite side of the front

107

Maroon Raglan Jacket

This jacket is much more of a sewn garment constructed from a fabric which has been treated to a felting process. The fascination of this garment was that the stitch pattern used was the same one used for the blue and red cape. It was 200 stitches wide and 450 rows long. However, where the cape was made from double-bed fabric, this fabric was single-bed Fair Isle fabric and the results of using a pattern like this on the single bed are fascinating! Because the floats are so long, the fabric does not remain flat and even but is distorted and gathered. The surface becomes very sculptured (Photo 61). In fact, the floats formed such an interesting pattern that it was very difficult to decide which side I wanted to use (Photo 62). Perhaps next time it will be the other side! The yarn used was a nice soft lamb's wool from Brockwell Wools, and I knitted up two sections for the front and came to a grinding halt. I had not decided beforehand what sort of garment I wanted to make from this fabric, and only knitted two sections mirroring the pattern. I made sure that they had enough extra felt at both ends of the pattern to give me enough room for manoeuvre when I did decide to cut it out. It was knitted over 200 stitches and 450 rows at tension 10 using a very fine yarn. The work was well weighted. The fronts used 175 g (6 oz) of tan and 425 g (15

oz) of maroon. I studied the fabric for a long time waiting for it to 'speak' to me and tell me what it wanted me to do with it. When you are stuck like that, often the best thing to do is to go away and leave it. When I came back and looked at the felted pieces again, they were upside down (or so I thought) but as an upside-down pattern they fitted beautifully into a raglan garment shape! The rest of the garment was plain and I used the maroon yarn and knitted it on the single bed to produce enough fabric when felted to cut out and sew the complete garment. It was knitted at tension 10 and produced a thick soft fabric which, in spite of its thickness, draped quite well and had a very 'sympathetic' feel. This only proves that all yarns react quite differently and unpredictably to the felting process.

I used a Vogue sewing pattern as a basis to start designing my garment. I altered the neckline and the collar because I wanted a small stand-up collar and the neckline needed to be higher to accommodate the pattern on the front of the garment pieces. Because of the floats I decided to line the garment but still used the technique of covering the edging with braid. This braid was knitted on the double bed as a full needle rib using one needle in the centre of the braid on one bed in non-working position to give a foldline. The braid was sewn on by hand. The garment was sewn up on the sewing machine and I included pockets in the side seams. One side was felted fabric, the other lining material. The seams were all top stitched to give the garment a crisper finish. The collar was two thicknesses of felt as this particular yarn did not result in a very stiff felted fabric and the collar would not have been stiff enough to stand up if it had only been one thickness of fabric (see colour pages).

61. *The front of a felted jacket, using single-bed Fair Isle*

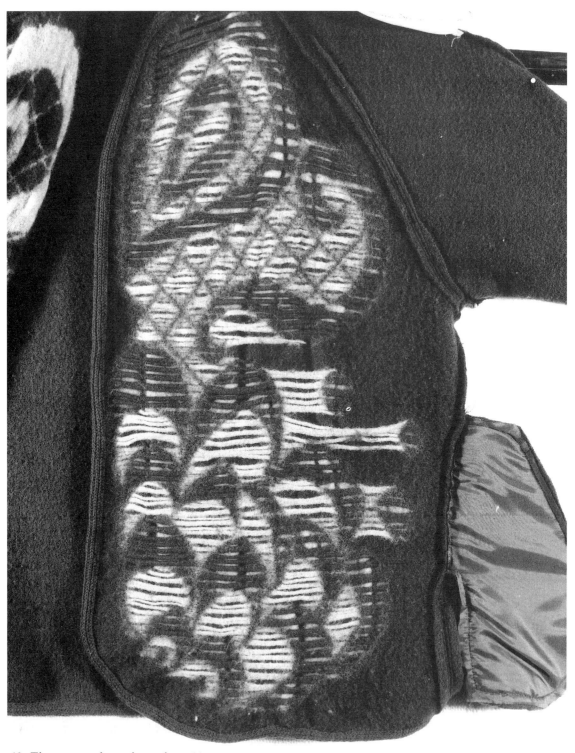

62. The reverse of sample in photo 61

Waistcoat

The stitch pattern or design for this garment was based on visual research done on African costume and ornament. In fact the concept of the pattern was adapted from a photograph of a beaded garment worn by a young African tribeswoman. The pattern was drawn out on a mylar sheet and knitted on an electronic knitting machine (Fig. 56). It is 60 stitches wide and 150 rows long.

Before a final decision was made about which technique to use to knit the fabric and which yarn to use, a number of swatches were knitted and then felted in the washing machine. All samples were knitted over 120 needles on the main bed and 150 pattern rows (Photo 63).

Sample 1 was knitted as a single-bed Fair Isle using tension 4. The two yarns used were a dark green pure wool and a lighter shade of green which was a wool mixed with 10% nylon. It was washed on a normal cycle with detergent and a plimsoll. The sample was sewn into a tube by hand using sewing cotton with the right sides together. After being in the washing machine it was dried in the tumble dryer for 20 minutes at a high heat. The sample measured 34 cm by 36 cm ($13\frac{1}{4} \times 14$ in.) before felting and 21 cm by 24.5 cm ($8\frac{1}{4} \times 9\frac{1}{2}$ in.) after being felted. The pure wool reacted better to the felting than the wool mix. The floats of the pure wool yarn felted very well and the wool knitting lost all appearance of individual stitches. It became a smooth amalgamated matt fabric. The mixed yarn did not felt as well. The floats did not felt and the stitches were still discernible in the knitted fabric. The long floats of pure wool did affect the surface finish of the fabric. The shrinkage gave the surface an interesting gathered sort of texture. The areas of wool mix seemed to be puckered by the pull of the shrunken floats of the pure wool.

When the same wool was used to knit a sample in double-bed jacquard using the same number of needles on the main or patterning bed and an equal number of needles on the opposite bed, quite a different result was produced. The same number of pattern rows were knitted, but as you have to move the carriage twice for every pattern row you knit, 300 rows were knitted in total at tension 4/4. A bigger stitch size was tried (6/6) but the fine wool only dropped stitches and when I tried to use weights to keep the knitting on the needles the fine wool broke. The fabric was knitted using a one-by-one or 'bird's eye' backing. The darker wool was very fine and delicate and tore easily so had to be cast on using a smaller stitch size. This particular pattern could not be knitted using a single colour backing (slipping the stitches on the ribber for two rows every two rows) because the pattern stitches were too far apart and the stitches dropped. The sample measured 38cm by 36 cm (15×14 in.) before being put into the washing machine and 28cm by 24 cm ($11 \times 9\frac{1}{2}$ in.) after felting. Here the effect of the non-felting of the wool mix was not at all noticeable and a very firm fabric with a nice handle was produced. You can still see the stitches of the wool mix knitted on the surface but there is no gathering or puckering effect. The fabric is much more homogeneous.

In the third sample the same technique was used but in this case, the wool mix was

63. (samples from the bottom left, anti-clockwise) Single-bed Fair Isle wool with a wool and nylon mix yarn; double-bed jacquard with a birds-eye backing, using the same yarns as the previous sample; double-bed jacquard with a birds-eye backing using wool and brite acrylic; release stitch using wool and acrylic; single-bed Fair Isle using wool and brite acrylic

combined with two strands of a brite acrylic. There was not much felting but there was some shrinkage. The fabric was also knitted using a one-by-one or 'bird's eye' backing and not striping. The tension was 4/4 and the same number of stitches and rows as the previous sample were knitted. The measurement of the swatch was 36 cm by 41 cm (14 × 16 in.) before processing in the washing machine and 34 cm by 33 cm ($13\frac{1}{4}$ × 13 in.) afterwards. It became narrower if not shorter, but felting was minimal.

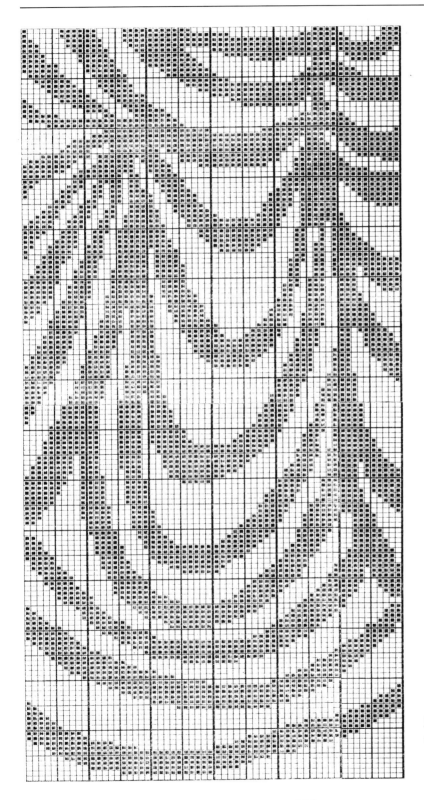

Fig. 56 Fair Isle stitch pattern
used in photo 63

The fourth sample was produced by the 'release stitch' method. An ordinary double-bed jacquard fabric was knitted over 120 needles on the main bed (the same on the ribber) and 300 rows using a striping background on the ribber. The tension was 4/4. When the knitting was complete, before removing the fabric from the machine, all the stitches were dropped off the *main bed* and run back down to the cast-on row. Then the stitches on the ribber were bound off. This produces a very light floaty fabric which must then be carefully prepared before it is put into the washing machine to be felted. It must be rolled up carefully in muslin so that it is completely enclosed and one part of the fabric does not come into contact with any other part of the fabric. The roll must then be securely fastened by sewing it up by hand with sewing cotton which can be removed when the process is complete. The parcel or roll is then put into the washing machine on an ordinary wash at 30°C (86°F) with a plimsoll or flip-flop and detergent or Sansolaine. This process will begin the amalgamating procedure. After the first wash it is removed from the machine and unrolled. If the fabric has not felted sufficiently it can now be placed back into the machine and re-processed without having to take the precautions of rolling it in muslin. In the finished fabric the wool will have felted beautifully and all traces of individual stitches will have vanished. The woollen knitting becomes felt while the acrylic yarn is not affected at all, giving an innovative and exciting fabric which is felt and yet not felt.

In the fifth and last sample I reverted again to single-bed Fair Isle, but I plied-up the yarn to make it much thicker, and I used two ends of pure wool and one end of wool-mix yarn in one feeder with two ends of brite acrylic in the second feeder. The sample was knitted over 120 needles and 150 at tension 8. It measured 36 cm by 41 cm (14 × 16 in.) before treatment and 25 cm by 37 cm (10 × 14½ in.) afterwards. The floats are a problem, and any garment made of this fabric would have to be lined, as the acrylic strands would catch on anything and everything. But the surface detailing of the fabric is fabulous. The felting of the wool has been impeded by the inclusion of the one strand of mixed yarn, but even so the result is very exciting indeed.

Ultimately I decided to play safe and opted to make a waistcoat out of the double-bed jacquard fabric knitted in the pure wool and wool-mix yarn. The waistcoat was designed around the pattern repeat with a central seam up the back to ensure a matching pattern. The front was knitted in two sections. The hem was merely cut cleanly using the stitch pattern as a guide for the shaping. After being felted in the washing machine at 30°C (86°F) on a normal wash with a plimsoll, the fabric was put into the tumble dryer for 10 minutes on hot. It was then pressed with a steam iron to set it and smooth it. It was cut out according to a very simple pattern and the edges were merely stay-stitched by hand on the wrong side using a fine sewing cotton to prevent any loss of shape or fluting (see colour pages).

By weighing the yarn both before and after the garment was made, I found I had used 225 g (8 oz) of dark green pure wool and 175 g (6 oz) of mid-green wool/nylon mix making a total of 400 g (14 oz) in all for the garment.

Fabric Paint on Felt

This garment illustrates how felting can be integrated into a garment along with sections of knitted fabric. The felt has also been embellished using a fabric paint/dye. In the first place the garment pattern had to be established. The design for the garment was created by using a 'design doll' (Photo 64). The doll was an accurate, two-dimensional fifth-scale model of the person for whom the garment was to be made. The outline of the garment was drawn around the design doll and then coloured. It was cut out with tabs at the shoulders so that it could be 'hung' onto the doll to help assess the appearance and fit of the garment and it could be viewed overall with a skirt. Then the basic block for the client was used to draft the pattern for the

64. Trying out the garment design on the design doll

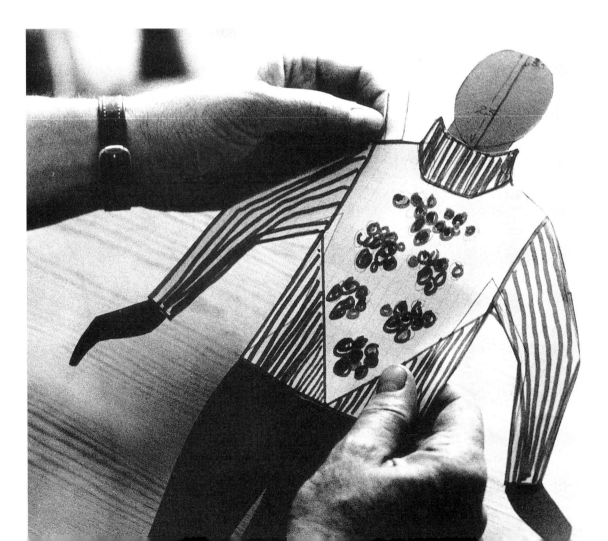

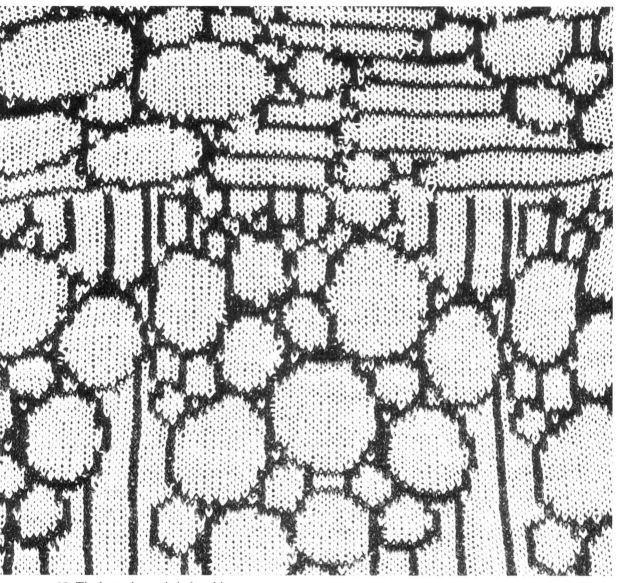

65. *The knitted sample before felting*

actual garment. Ease and design features such as the line for the felt inset and collar were added. The new block including these features was cut out. The pieces could now be used as a template for cutting out the finished piece of felt and also placed onto the knit radar/tracer/leader as a guide for knitting the ribbed sections of the garment such as the sleeves and side bodice sections.

Then the stitch pattern for the felted fabric was drawn out and transferred onto a pattern sheet for the electronic knitting machine (Fig. 57). A sample was knitted using one strand of fine white wool and one strand of fine dark purple wool as a single-bed Fair Isle pattern over 100 stitches and 100 rows at tension 4, and felted in the washing machine to help to determine how

116

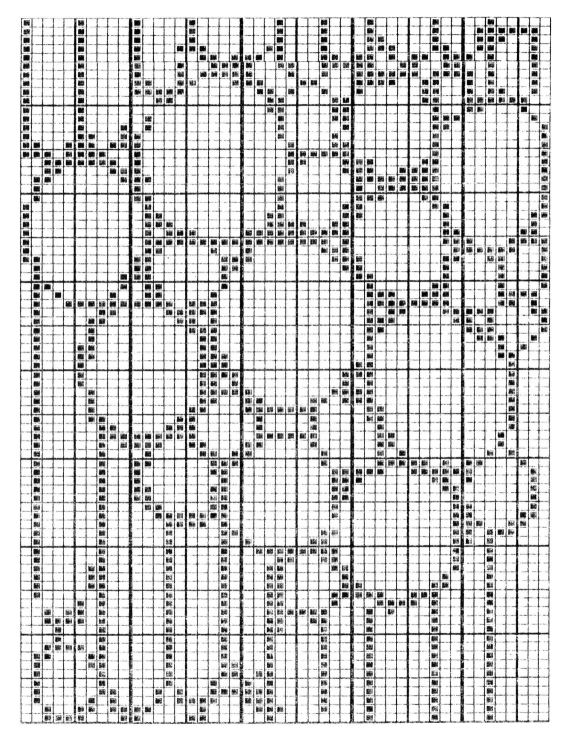

*Fig. 57 Fair Isle stitch pattern used with fabric
paint in photo 67*

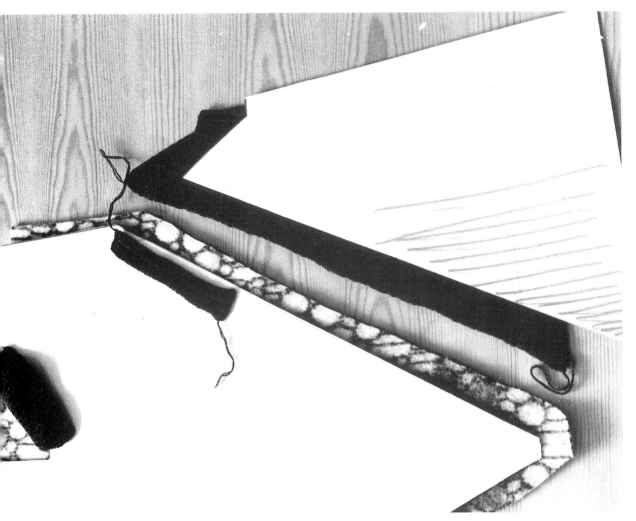

66. *Cutting the felt, and knitting the ribbing according to the garment pattern, plus samples for the collar and seam detailing*

many stitches and rows would be required for the garment pieces. The knitted sample measured 24 cm wide by 21.5 cm long (9½ × 8½ in.) before processing (Photo 65). After being in the washing machine, the sample measured 18 cm wide and 15.3 cm long. (7 × 6 in.).

The felted sample was then painted with Roy Russell's 'Cool Wool Dyes'. One teaspoon of dye powder was dissolved in two teaspoons of hot water. The liquid was then painted onto the dry felt, so that the area was well saturated with colour. The sample was then rolled up in cling film and left wet for 24 hours. This gives the dye time to go 'off' and makes it fast to light and washing. The sample was then rinsed through until all traces of dye were rinsed away and the water ran clear. The dye did not migrate into other (unwanted) areas of felt but remained fast in the area that had been painted (see colour pages).

Having done all the experimenting on the sample I was now ready to knit the fabric.

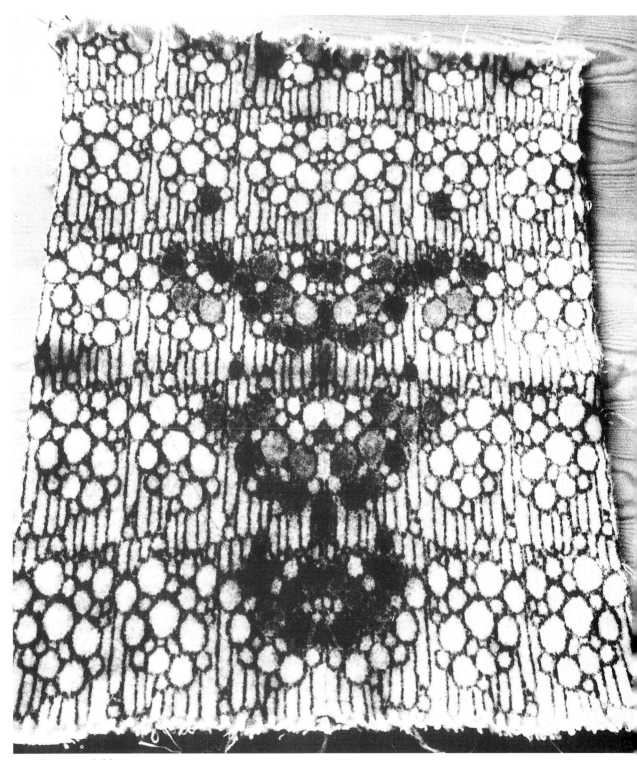

67. The painted felt

The front as well as the back were knitted in pairs which were then joined up in the middle. One side was knitted and then the stitch pattern was reversed to give a mirror image when the second side was knitted. When they were removed from the knitting machine, they were steamed with a steam iron to flatten them. The two pieces were joined on a linker using the same yarn. They were each then sewn together loosely around the edges by hand using sewing cotton to form an envelope. The two 'envelopes' were put into the washing machine at a normal cycle of 30°C (86°F), half load with half a cup of detergent and two plimsolls. After they were removed from the machine, the envelopes were tumbled dry for 10 minutes on high heat and then the edges were cut open. They were pressed flat and allowed to dry. They were then painted, rolled up in cling film and left for 24 hours. The ribbing for the garment was knitted on tension 1/1 according to the garment shape required. When the dye had 'gone off', the felt was washed and dried and the shape required for the pattern was cut out (Photo 66). The front and back were sewn together on the sewing machine and trimmed around the edge with a hand-sewn braid which had been knitted on the machine using the purple yarn. The braid was a full needle rib with one needle in non-working position in the middle on one bed to give a foldline.

The collar was also knitted using the ribber and both stitch structure and stitch size were adjusted to graduate the width of the fabric. A racking cast-on was used to make it very loose, then English rib (half tuck) stitch structure was used starting with tension 4/4 and gradually making the stitch size smaller and smaller. The last rows were knitted as an ordinary rib at tension 2/2. The collar was then scrapped off the machine onto waste yarn and sewn onto the garment by hand. This gives the collar a nice roll.

The important thing to remember about this garment is the careful planning that went into every stage of its construction: first the garment design; then the actual garment pattern; and finally (and most important) the sample swatches for every bit of fabric and variation that went into the making up of the garment. The following samples were made: of the felt, painted (Photo 67); of the ribbing for the sides of the bodice and the sleeves; of the braid for the edging; and finally for the collar. You must practise on the samples, not on the garment!

White Tops

I fell in love with the felted release-stitch fabric. I thought it would look wonderful on a garment, but where to use it? There are lots of possibilities – sleeves, full skirts, draped long dresses – but I thought it might be an idea if I started out modestly, so perhaps it would lend itself to a full draped dramatic collar on a neat jacket? I could use the motif from the collar which would be made in release stitch as a motif for a traditional double-bed jacquard fabric which would make up the body of the jacket. I had a

68. Planning a pattern

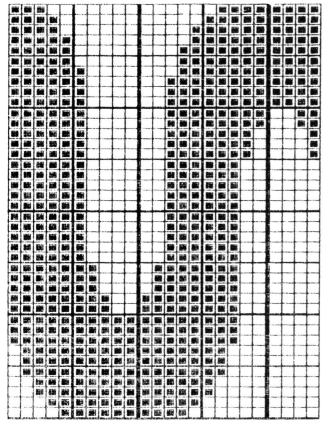

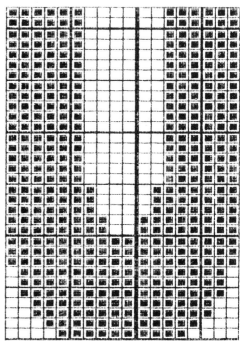

Fig. 58 Fair Isle stitch pattern for use as motif

Fig. 59 Fair Isle stitch pattern shown in photo 68

number of motifs that were suitable. Simple geometric shapes would be very striking knitted either as release-stitch felted fabric or as double-bed jacquard felted fabric using a combination of pure fine wool with acrylic. I tried combining the acrylic with a fancy glitter yarn and I tried knitting the swatch in coloured yarns but I was not keen on the effect. In the end I settled for white on white; a simple, subtle solution. I like the idea of a simple circle. Then I tried a 'polo', a circle with a hole in the middle. That was even more interesting. If you cut that motif in half and move it about, the permutations are amazing (Photo 68)!

I began to play with cut-out pieces of paper and developed a number of design ideas. It was quite simple to put these on a punch card or a pattern sheet for an electronic machine and try them out (Figs. 58–60). I drafted out a simple garment shape by adding length, and ease to the bust, dropping the armhole a bit and putting a 'V' neckline on my basic body block. I then divided it up the middle front and drafted a sleeve to make a jacket pattern. I cut out the pattern shapes in a fine wadding and sewed them together carefully by hand to try the shape on. The wadding simulated the bulk and stiffness of the felted fabric and gave me quite a good idea of what the finished garment would look like. (This idea was first used by Kathy Duffee when she adapted a pattern from a jacket she already had, as she was intending to make a quilted garment.)

From my knitted swatch I knew how

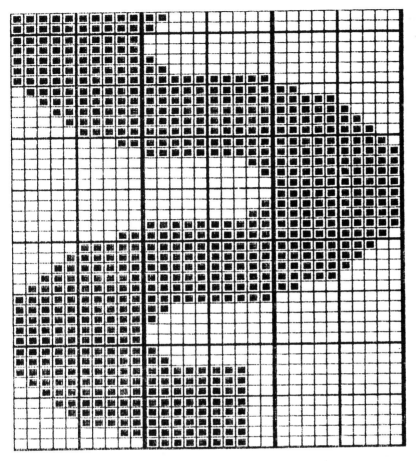

Fig. 60 Fair Isle stitch pattern for use as motif

many stitches and rows I needed to knit to give me a piece of fabric large enough to cut out my two front sections. I knitted these two pieces in double-bed jacquard using wool as the main yarn and acrylic as the contrast yarn. But when I got them out of the washing machine, although they had felted quite well, I realized the proportion of pattern area to plain did not give me a fabric which would be suitable to make the type of jacket I had in mind. Disaster! I casually threw the two pieces over my 'model' and went back to the drawing board to re-design the fabric stitch pattern, isolating the motifs more on the background.

When I looked back at my model, I thought it might be a good idea to play

around with the two knitted sections. I folded them here and pinned them there and lo and behold I had created a very interesting top (Photo 69). All I needed was to knit a section of ribbing to fill in at the back. Using a piece of fine lining fabric, I pinned it onto the front and drew out the shape I needed for the back ribbed inset. Then I knitted a tension swatch for full needle rib on tension 0/0. I knitted the piece of ribbing and made the required shape using the cut-and-sew technique. This was then sewn into the back section, and a plain braid knitted in the acrylic yarn on the single-bed machine was used to finish off the collar and front edge of the garment. So a disaster was turned into a victory, and I discovered the joys of draping

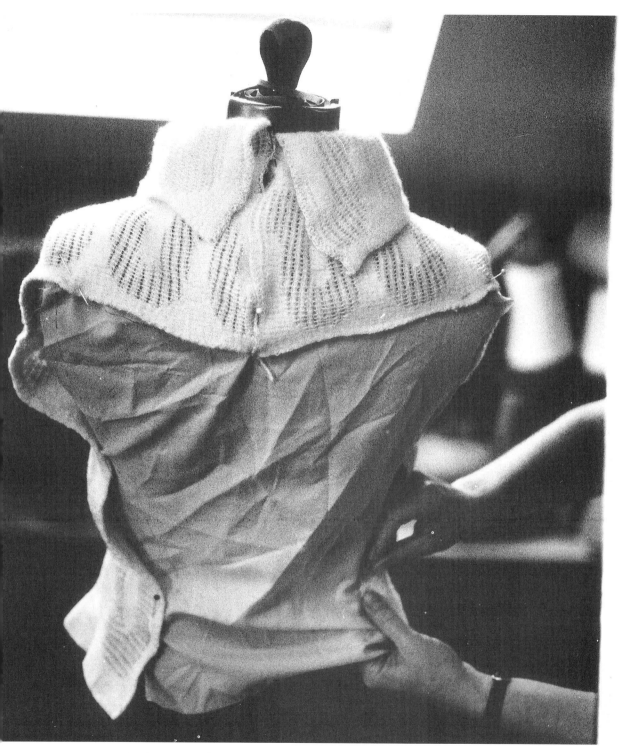

69. *Draping the felting on a dummy*

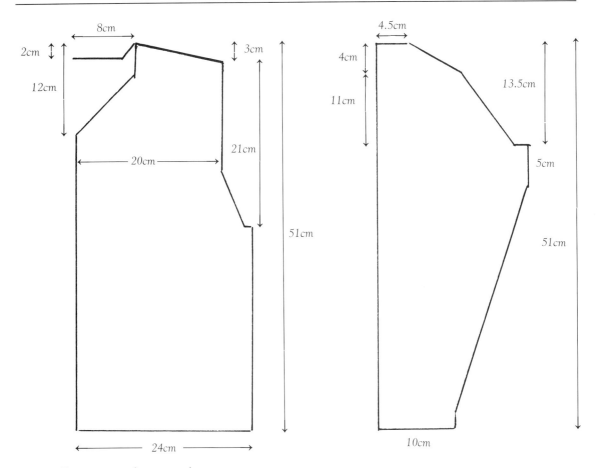

Fig. 61 Dimensions of garment shapes

fabric on the body to create garment shapes that might never have emerged had I just relied on flat pattern cutting to generate garment design.

Having produced a very interesting variation on my theme, I then returned to the original idea, which was a jacket with a release-stitch collar. I had the collar and all I had to do was to produce the fabric for the jacket. With the revised pattern I found the felt was entirely suitable for making a short neat jacket (Fig. 61). I used an overlocking machine to finish off the edges of the felt fabric because it would give a neater and more professional finish. There was no fear that the acrylic element of the fabric would

run because the felted wool would hold it in place. The garment was then assembled on the sewing machine. The collar was gathered and sewn around the neck edge. Two strips of stocking-stitch knitting the width of the machine and approximately 12 rows long was knitted and sewn on by hand onto the front edges of the jacket and around the neck edge over the collar. Small shoulder pads completed the tailored look (see colour pages).

From one design idea and one design motif I had produced two entirely different garments and had enough food for thought to go on producing many more.

Bibliography

Helen Bennett, *Scottish Knitting*, Shire Album No. 164, 1986
M.E. Burkett, *The Art of the Felt Maker*, Abbot Hall Art Gallery, Kendal, Cumbria, 1979
Raymonde Chessum, *How to Make Felt Material on Your Knitting Machine*, Metropolitan St. No. 838
Marlie Claessen, *Felting*, Louet BV Lochem, Holland, 1981
J. Gordon Cook, *Handmade Textile Fibres*, Merrow, 1959–68
Arved Datyner, *Surfactants in Textile Processing*, Marcel Dekker, 1983
Kay Donald, *Creative Feltmaking*, Kangaroo Press, 1983

Inge Evers, *Felt Making Technique and Projects!* A.C. Blade, 1987
Sue Freeman, *Felt Craft*, David & Charles, 1988
Nance B. Keenan, *The Boiled Wool Jacket and Vest*, A. Raphael Knitte, 1985
Nance B. Keenan, *Boiled Wool for the Bulky Machine*, Outdoors Weight, A. Raphael Knitte, 1986
Ewa Kuniczak-Coles, 'Felt Making-Washing Machine Method', in *Textiles, Chemicals and Auxiliaries*, ed. Speel & Schwarz, Reinhold Pub., 1957
Deborah Newton, 'Fulling' in *Vogue Knitting*, Autumn/Winter 1985/86

W.J. Onions, *Wool, an Introduction to its Properties, Varieties, Uses and Production*, Interscience, 1962
Mary Smith, 'Boiled Wool' in *Threads*, Oct./Nov. 1987
Patricia Spark, *Fundamentals of Feltmaking*, Shuttle Craft Books, USA, 1989
E.R. Trotman, *Dyeing and Chemical Technology of Textile Fibres*, Griffin, 1984
A.E. Vickrey, *Felting by Hand*, Craft Works Publishing, USA, 1951

Suppliers

Punch for rag rugs:
Jenni Stuart-Anderson
The Birches
Middleton-on-the-Hill
Herefordshire HR6 0HZ
Tel: Leysters (056 887) 229

Sansolaine low-sudsing detergent:
Brockwell Wools
Stansfield Mill
Stansfield Mill Lane
Triangle
Sowerby Bridge
West Yorkshire HX6 3LZ

M & R Dyes:
Carters
Station Road
Wickham Bishops
Witham
Essex CM8 3JB
Tel: Maldon (0621) 891405

Index

Index